ASYMMETRIC CONFLICT

ISRAEL-LEBANON WAR, 2006

ASYMMETRIC CONFLICT
ISRAEL-LEBANON WAR, 2006

Col Harjeet Singh

PENTAGON PRESS

ASYMMETRIC CONFLICT: ISRAEL-LEBANON WAR, 2006

Col Harjeet Singh

ISBN 978-93-86618-24-5

First Published in 2018

The views and opinions expressed in this book are the author's, as well as the facts reported by him. The Publisher is in no way liable for the same. No responsibility for loss caused to any individual or organisation acting, or refraining from action, as a result of the material in this book can be accepted by Pentagon Press or the Author.

All maps in this book are purely representative and do not depict correct national boundaries.

Published by
PENTAGON PRESS
206, Peacock Lane, ShahpurJat
New Delhi-110049
Phones: 011-64706243, 26491568
Telefax: 011-26490600
email: rajan@pentagonpress.in
website: www.pentagonpress.in

Printed at Avantika Printers Private Limited.

Contents

MAPS AND SKETCHES

TABLES

PHOTOS

ABBREVIATIONS

ATGM	Antitank Guided Missile
APC	Armoured Personnel Carrier
C2	Command and Control
C2ISR	Command and Control, Intelligence, Surveillance, and Reconnaissance
C-SIGNET	Counter-Signals Intelligence
COIN	Counterinsurgency
COMINT	Communications Intelligence
COS	Chief of Staff
DoD	Department of Defence
DOTMLPF	Doctrine, Organisation, Training, Materiel, Leadership and Education, Personnel, and Facilities
EBO	Effects-based Operations
ERA	Explosive Reactive Armour
FCS	Future Combat Systems
GPS	Global Positioning System
HEAT	High Explosive Anti-Tank
HIC	High-Intensity Conflict
HMMWV	High Mobility Multi-Purpose Wheeled Vehicle
HUMINT	Human Intelligence
HVT	High-Value Target
IAF	Israeli Air Force
IDF	Israel Defence Forces
IED	Improvised Explosive Device
IO	Information Operations

IR	Islamic Resistance
ISR	Intelligence, Surveillance, and Reconnaissance
IW	Irregular Warfare
JFAC	Joint Forward Air Control
JFCOM	US Joint Forces Command
JTAC	Joint Tactical Air Control
LAF	Lebanese Armed Forces
LIC	Low-Intensity Conflict
MANPADS	Man-Portable Air-Defence System
MBT	Main Battle Tank
MCO	Major Combat Operations
MRAP	Mine-Resistant Ambush-Protected Vehicle
NA	Not Available
NCW	Network-Centric Warfare
OTRI	Operational Theory Research Institute
PA	Palestinian Authority
PGM	Precision Guided Munition
PIJ	Palestinian Islamic Jihad
PLO	Palestine Liberation Organisation
RMA	Revolution in Military Affairs
RPG	Rocket-Propelled Grenade
SEAD	Suppression of Enemy Air Defences
SIGINT	Signals Intelligence
SLA	South Lebanon Army
SOD	Systemic Operational Design
SSM	Surface-to-Surface Missile
TTP	Tactics, Techniques, and Procedures
UAV	Unmanned Aerial Vehicle
UN	United Nations
UNIFIL	United Nations Interim Force in Lebanon
UNSCR	United Nations Security Council Resolution
US	United States of America

INTRODUCTION

War in the 21st century is increasingly witnessing the phenomenon of asymmetric warfare between combatants of unequal military power. This is exemplified by the continuing *mujahideen* war in Afghanistan and Hezbollah's insurgency against Israel's occupation of South Lebanon for more than 20 years. Lebanon is no stranger to conflict. Due to a mix of weak political institutions, internal sectarian political divisions, and deep and often aggressive foreign intervention, the small Mediterranean country has time and time again oscillated between war and peace, stability and chaos, for the past decades.

Most wars in the 21st century have not been terminated with realistic hopes of quick resolution of the underlying reasons for the conflict. The war between Hezbollah and Israel added another round to the agonies of the Arab-Israeli conflict, ending with a fragile situation along the Israeli-Lebanese border. The war also brought the general confrontation between the West and Islamic fundamentalism to include a new theatre of operations. The 2006 Lebanon War was not just another interlude of the Arab-Israeli conflict. Departing from the familiar pattern of classic warfare, it was a sub-conventional, asymmetric war between Israel and Hezbollah, a non-state, irregular force waging a guerrilla war.

The 2006 Lebanon War, also known in Israel as the Second Lebanon War was a 34-day military conflict in Lebanon, Northern Israel and the Golan Heights. The principal parties were Hezbollah paramilitary forces and the Israel Defence Forces (IDF). The conflict started on 12 July 2006, and continued until a United Nations-brokered ceasefire went into effect in the morning on 14 August 2006, though it formally ended on 8 September 2006 when Israel lifted its naval blockade of Lebanon. Due to unprecedented Iranian military support to Hezbollah before and during the war, some consider it the first round of the Iran–Israel proxy conflict, rather than a continuation of the Arab–Israeli conflict.

The Second Lebanon War embodied a military confrontation different from the many other clashes that Israel has engaged in since its establishment as a nation-state. This confrontation falls in the category of asymmetrical wars involving rival entities endowed with inherently different and unbalanced attributes. Israel, a sovereign state with a strong, organised military, faced Hezbollah, a sub-state organisation that operated from within a failed state while controlling a relatively small guerrilla force. Size notwithstanding, the force boasted considerable military abilities and was well positioned for this type of confrontation. Hezbollah presented Israel with a stiff challenge, built on years of painstaking preparation and close Iranian support. It displayed a strategic concept that maximised its abilities and compensated for its weaknesses in the face of a stronger rival. Although in this kind of confrontation it is difficult to identify victor or victory definitively, it is clear that, in view of the expectations and perceptions in Israel, the opinions in the Arab world, and the outlook of the global community, Hezbollah achieved prominent and tangible achievements, while Israel emerged from the confrontation bruised and disappointed.

The history of Lebanon in the conflict has been especially complex. The countdown to the war began with the shocking political assassination, on 14 February 2005, of twice-Prime Minister, Rafiq al-Hariri. Lebanon is still coping with the legacy of that event, even though much has happened since, including the war with Israel in the summer of 2006 and, more recently, the destabilising effect of the civil conflict in Syria. Yet the roots of Lebanon's current political crisis can be traced back to that event.

The period following the Hariri assassination ushered in the Independence *Intifada* (or Cedar Revolution), the protests that put an end to the Syrian military presence in Lebanon, in April 2005. However, the Syrian legacy in the country went far deeper than its military presence. It was soon discovered that any effort to alter the country's political outlook significantly would encounter deep and entrenched resistance. Lebanon thus settled for an uneasy balance between pro- and anti-Damascus sentiments.

The Cedar Revolution also saw the rise of two largely antagonistic political blocs—the March 14 revolutionary forces and the March 8 resistance camp. The former, led by al-Hariri's son Saad, head of the *Tayyar al-Mustaqbal* (Future Movement), a political party that largely represents Lebanon's Sunni community is favoured by the West and backed by Saudi Arabia. The resistance camp, on the other hand, is led by Hezbollah and supported by Iran and Syria, and speaks for the country's Shiites. With the Lebanese Maronite Christian community more or less evenly divided across the two sides, the March 14 and March 8 blocs reflect rooted and divergent political, sectarian, and geostrategic interests. The Syrian civil war has only worsened this dynamic by further entrenching the deep animosity, mutual distrust, and parochialism of both sides. The inability of the counterpoising camps to work together has led to a series of political crises and domestic strife, and, ultimately, to deep political paralysis.

The 2006 Lebanon War broke out without either Israel or Hezbollah intending this escalation. However, the abduction of IDF soldiers by a Hezbollah cell prompted Israel to embark on a military operation, which ultimately became a war. The course and outcomes of the war strongly affected subsequent internal and external Israeli, Lebanese, and regional processes.

The conflict was precipitated by a Hezbollah cross-border raid. On 12 July 2006, Hezbollah fighters fired rockets at Israeli border towns as a diversion for an anti-tank missile attack on two armoured Humvees patrolling the Israeli side of the border fence. The ambush left three soldiers dead. Two Israeli soldiers were abducted and taken by Hezbollah to Lebanon. Five more were killed in Lebanon, in a failed rescue attempt. Hezbollah demanded the release of Lebanese prisoners held by Israel in exchange for the release of the abducted soldiers. Israel refused and responded with airstrikes and artillery fire on targets in Lebanon. Israel attacked both Hezbollah military targets and Lebanese civilian infrastructure, including Beirut's International Airport. The IDF then launched a ground invasion of Southern Lebanon. Israel also imposed an air and naval blockade. Hezbollah then launched more rockets into northern Israel and engaged the IDF in guerrilla warfare from hardened positions. The conflict is believed to have killed between 1,191 and 1,300 Lebanese (mostly civilians), and 165 Israelis (including 44 civilians). It severely damaged Lebanese civil infrastructure, and displaced approximately one million Lebanese and 300,000–500,000 Israelis.

Hindsight provides an opportunity to examine the war and its ramifications from a broader and more balanced perspective. Studying the past and learning its lessons gives a better understanding of the subsequent decade, sheds light on the current state of Israel's northern sector, and contributes to an assessment of possible future scenarios.

For Israel, the Second Lebanon War was a milestone in several ways. It was the first war in which Israel was exposed to the massive use of high trajectory fire directed at its civilian population. The central role played by the civilian front in the fighting brought some new critical issues to the fore. The protection of national infrastructures, the level of national resilience, the functional continuity of critical systems, and the Israeli economy will be basic components of any future campaign.

The eve of the Second Lebanon War caught the IDF at a low level of preparedness and with a new operational doctrine that was not widely understood or assimilated by the fighting forces. After six years, during which the IDF devoted its effort and attention primarily to fighting terrorism in Judea, Samaria, and the Gaza Strip, it suddenly found itself in a new situation in Lebanon which forced it, for the first time since the 1982 Lebanon War, to adapt and adjust rapidly to fighting a war in which it had to combine ground manoeuvre with standoff fire. The war compelled the IDF to re-examine its force build-up and operational doctrine, improve the army's basic skills, refresh the way in which the reserves are employed, and give new thought to emergency stockpiles.

Another aspect that was unique to the war was its exposure by the media. New technologies allowed the media to cover the war and provide public access to the events in near real-time. There was round the clock coverage from the battlefield, often facilitated by the soldiers themselves. The depiction of the events in the media played a large role in the war of perception waged alongside the kinetic war. That depiction—the images of the war and the public's opinion of the war that was crafted—often eclipsed the actual war.

The war was a milestone for Hezbollah as well. In the years leading up to 2006, it coasted on its popularity as the organisation that managed to eject the IDF from southern Lebanon. During the war it established itself as a military outfit with some features of regular forces, capable of fighting the army that is considered the strongest in the Middle East. However, Hezbollah's image as the protector of Lebanon was shattered as a result of the vast damage the war inflicted on the country. Furthermore, the war increased Iranian supervision of Hezbollah.

Perhaps, the event with the greatest impact is the civil war in Syria, with its vast flood of refugees, coupled with terrorism in both urban and rural areas, Hezbollah's intervention to help Bashar Assad in the civil war, and the consequent effect on Lebanon. As the war in Syria drags on, and as Hezbollah has managed to prevent it from trickling across the border into Lebanon, the organisation's status has risen once again and its image as the protector of Lebanon stands restored.

Israel's northern arena has changed greatly. The Syrian civil war has resulted in fluctuating power balances and even a role reversal: the Golan Heights, which was Israel's calmest border over four decades, has become a highly volatile hive of activity on the Syrian side, whereas southern Lebanon, which was a battlefield for several decades, has been calm since 2006. The Second Lebanon War played a central role in creating the current equation between Israel and Hezbollah (and its allies), where the mutual desire is to prevent extensive escalation.

The starting assumption of many Israelis is that the countdown to the Third Lebanon War has already begun. The fact that Hezbollah is arming itself for a future war is indisputable. The organisation is fine-tuning its capabilities and gaining combat experience on the battlefields of Syria. In parallel, the IDF of today has imbibed its lessons, and a new war is liable to inflict on Lebanon much more extensive and intensive damage than it suffered in 2006. Therefore, the challenge facing Israel's decision-makers is neither the number of missiles in Hezbollah's arsenal, nor the need to repair the IDF's tarnished image and somehow make up for the widespread sense that an opportunity was missed. Rather, the challenge is to prevent another widespread confrontation, reduce Hezbollah's force construction, and build the capabilities needed to severely damage the organisation when the opportunity presents itself.

On 11 August 2006, the United Nations Security Council unanimously approved Resolution 1701 (UNSCR 1701) in an effort to end the hostilities. The resolution, which was approved by both the Lebanese and Israeli governments, called for disarmament of Hezbollah, for withdrawal of the IDF from Lebanon, and for the deployment of the Lebanese Armed Forces and an enlarged United Nations Interim Force in Lebanon (UNIFIL) in the south. UNIFIL has an expanded mandate, including the ability to use force to ensure that its area of responsibility is not used for hostile activities, and to resist attempts by force to prevent them from discharging their duties. The Lebanese Army began deploying in Southern Lebanon on 17 August 2006. The blockade was lifted on 8 September 2006. On 1 October 2006, most Israeli troops withdrew from Lebanon, although the last of the troops continued to occupy the border-straddling village of Ghajar. In the time since the enactment of UNSCR 1701 both the Lebanese government and UNIFIL have stated that they will not disarm Hezbollah. The remains of the two captured soldiers, whose fates were unknown, were returned to Israel on 16 July 2008 as part of a prisoner exchange.

Although in some ways a limited war between Israel and a non-state actor in one Arab country, the 2006 Lebanon War had a large impact on politics and power perceptions in the region comparable to the effects of larger and wider wars. It was the first war that did not end in victory for Israel; it was the first Iranian proxy war against Israel; it was the first large-scale Islamist war against Israel; it was another partial defeat for US policy; and it showed up new ways of confronting Israel. Although the human and socio-economic damage to Israel was barely 5 percent of the damage to Lebanon, the war had enormous political and military impacts on Israel.

Although most Israelis started off supporting the war, they ended up deeply dissatisfied with the conduct of the war, and the war ended with most Israelis feeling that Israel—while perhaps not losing outright, had not won the war, and its nemesis, Hezbollah, had survived and had even scored a number of victories, continuing to launch rockets into Israel throughout the war, and defeating Israeli tank and infantry columns on the battlefield. A nation that believes that it cannot afford to lose any war was deeply distressed by the inconclusive results of the 2006 Lebanon War. Thus, with Israeli expectations high of victory in every battle and every war, the mixed result of the war was perceived as a loss. For Hezbollah, surviving the Israeli onslaught and simply being able to continue to fight throughout the war was interpreted around the Arab and Islamic world as a victory.

From the Israeli perspective, at the political level, the conduct of the war discredited the leadership of the country—Prime Minister Ehud Olmert, Defence Minister Amir Peretz, and Israeli Defence Forces Chief Dan Halutz, who resigned in mid-January 2007.

Beyond the military aspect, the war between Israel and Hezbollah reflected a number of strategic processes essential to understanding the general regional picture: the strengthening of Islamic radicalism and its evolution into an active anti-status quo power; the weakening of the Arab states; the growth of non-state actors that exploit the weakness of the state system; and the difficulties faced by the international community in coping with these processes.

From the outset of the war, opinion in the Arab media varied between support for Hezbollah and condemnations of its behaviour as irresponsible and as having led to a deteriorated state of security in Lebanon. The voice of the Arab street, however was clear in supporting Nasrallah and his militia. As soon as the war broke out, protests shook Arab streets, with Hezbollah banners held high. Islamic sentiments were mobilised for the struggle with Israel and became a rallying cry in support of Hezbollah. Some newspapers distributed free posters of Nasrallah, depicting him as "the symbol of resistance," and bumper stickers with his picture began to appear on cars in the Arab streets.

Moreover, as soon as UNSCR 1701 was adopted and the cease-fire began to be implemented, Arab newspapers and television channels became even more excited—and celebratory with respect to the "victorious" Arab militia. The main point was Israel's failure, despite its supreme military capability, to abolish an entity like Hezbollah. Nasrallah's personal survival was itself a focal point in these arguments, which portrayed the war as a failed Israeli manhunt for the movement's leader. The fact that the war did not end in Hezbollah's being compelled to disarm was another dimension of this narrative.

It seems that what propelled all of these arguments was an expectation that had come to dominate the Arab psyche (and perhaps the Israeli psyche as well) to the effect that any military confrontation with Israel would result in an opponent's absolute defeat and destruction. The fact that the war did not end with Hezbollah being wiped out was viewed as tantamount to Arab "Godly Victory," in Nasrallah's own words.

How should defeat and victory under conditions of asymmetrical warfare be evaluated? Is it possible to devise measures for evaluating the outcome of such confrontations? Israel would be seen as having won the war as decisively as victory can be defined under the conditions of asymmetrical warfare. Some yardsticks would be:

(a) The costs incurred by Israel were far lower than those incurred by its adversaries.

(b) Prime Minister Olmert is not the only leader who should be judged by the objectives he set. Hassan Nasrallah also posited objectives that were not met. He failed to fructify his claims that he would bring about the release of Arab prisoners; spearhead the liberation of Palestine; he would wage an open war against Israel; and he would "liberate" the Shebaa Farms.

(c) The Israeli government was criticised because a million of its citizens needed to find refuge in shelters. At least, it provided its citizens with such shelters. By contrast, Nasrallah failed to protect his people. Half a million Lebanese were displaced; more than a thousand were killed.

(d) At the end of the war, Israel held Lebanese territory; it maintained an air and sea quarantine of Lebanon; it held Lebanese prisoners; and it enjoyed the support of the international community—expressed in UNSCR 1701, which tilted clearly in Israel's favour. By contrast, Nasrallah held two Israeli soldiers and became the focus of anger on the part of the non-Shi'ite Lebanese.

(e) Hezbollah lost much of its stockpile of *Zilzal* and *Fagr* strategic missiles. By contrast, Israel lost none of its strategic assets.

The Israel-Lebanon war was also characterised by massive miscalculations on both sides. Hezbollah grossly miscalculated the Israeli response to the 12 July attack and the kidnapping of its two soldiers. Apparently, Nasrallah and his top aides did not take notice of the Israeli reaction to a similar operation by Palestinian forces, which had triggered a mini-war in Gaza just weeks earlier. A greater miscalculation was with respect to the international and regional—and Arab in particular—response to the kidnapping. Hezbollah thus overestimated its power and ability to lead not only Lebanon but the Arab world at large. Hassan Nasrallah also overestimated the ability of the Arab street to mobilise for a regional war. And this was in turn connected to his failure to clearly articulate the strategic purposes of the kidnapping.

Israel miscalculated massively even when its objectives were well defined. Israel failed to recognise that the absence of a serious peace process would eventually lead to one sort of war or another. The developments in

Gaza and Lebanon are symptoms of a protracted conflict that continues to fester over time and produce new mutations. Also, having had a large military presence in Lebanon for many years, Israel should have known that in a strategic environment like Lebanon, victory is not a well-defined concept that reflects the realities of power on the ground. Lebanon, after all, though it is the weakest and most fragile Arab country, was the only Arab country from which Israel was forced to withdraw in May 2000 without a peace treaty or security arrangements.

Israel also failed to evaluate the difficulties experienced by the US and others in Afghanistan and Iraq in facing insurgencies. It also miscalculated the response of the Lebanese people. It assumed that massive destruction of Lebanese human and material resources would cause the Lebanese people to direct their anger against Hezbollah. However, the Lebanese directed their anger at Israel, because they did not understand why Lebanon's destruction was an appropriate price to be paid for the abduction of two soldiers by Hezbollah. Moreover, the Lebanese people preferred to find themselves embroiled in war with Israel than in another civil war of their own. In short, the war humbled the bravado of both sides, notwithstanding their domestically motivated declarations of victory. Israel will also have to ask itself whether the war's gains justify its costs.

On the surface, it would appear that the 2006 Arab-Israeli war came and went like the previous wars, and numerous other confrontations, that have befallen the Middle East for more than half a century. Largely unnoticed, however, is the fact that the war between Hezbollah and Israel took place in a changed international and regional context. The regional environment is significantly affected by the growing influence of Islamic fundamentalism. The international environment has been transformed by the horrific 11 September 2001, terror attacks on the US. As a result of these dramatic changes, the stakes involved in any Arab-Israeli conflict are now greater than they have been at any time since October 1973, when the two superpowers found themselves on the brink of a nuclear confrontation. This new environment requires a reassessment of the political and strategic situation in the Middle East, and of the regional and global policies that have so far produced neither stability nor peace.

BACKGROUND

Lebanese National Pact

Lebanon was ruled by the Ottoman Empire from 1516 to 1918. Following the collapse of the empire after World War I, the five provinces that constitute modern Lebanon came under the French Mandate of Lebanon. The French expanded the borders of Lebanon, which was mostly populated by Maronites and Druze, to include more Muslims. Lebanon gained independence in 1943.

The Lebanese National Pact (*al Mithaq al Watani*), an unwritten agreement came into being in the summer of 1943, as a power-sharing arrangement between Lebanese Christians and Muslims. It laid the foundation of Lebanon as a multi-faith state, and has shaped the country to this day. It allowed Lebanon to be independent, following negotiations between the Shia, Sunni, and Maronite leaderships. The key points of the National Pact include:

- Maronite Christians would not seek foreign intervention, and accepted an Arab-affiliated Lebanon, instead of a Western one.
- Muslims abandoned their aspirations to unite with Syria.
- The President of the Republic is always a Maronite Catholic.
- The Prime Minister of the Republic is always a Sunni Muslim.
- The Speaker of the Parliament is always a Shia Muslim.
- The Deputy Speaker of the Parliament and the Deputy Prime Minister are always Greek Orthodox Christian.
- The Chief of the General Staff of the Armed Forces is always a Maronite Catholic.

- The Commander of the Lebanese Army is always a Druze.
- Parliament members are always in a ratio of 6:5 in favour of Christians to Muslims.

At the heart of the negotiations was the Christians' fear of being overwhelmed by the Muslim communities in Lebanon and the surrounding Arab countries, and the Muslims' fear of Western hegemony. In return for the Christian promise not to seek foreign, i.e., French protection and to accept Lebanon's "Arab face," the Muslim side agreed to recognise the independence and legitimacy of the Lebanese state in its 1920 boundaries and to renounce aspirations for union with Syria. A Christian majority of 51% in the 1932 census—widely considered manipulated in their favour—was the underpinning of a government structure that gave the Christians control of the presidency, command of the armed forces, and a parliamentary majority. However, the generally poorer Muslim population increased faster than the richer Christians. Additionally, the Christians emigrated in large numbers, further eroding their only marginal population edge, and it soon became clear that Christians wielded a disproportionate amount of power. As years passed without a new census, dissatisfaction with the government structure and sectarian rifts increased, eventually sparking the Lebanese Civil War, which continued from 1975 to 1990.

The Palestine Liberation Organisation

Cross-border attacks from southern Lebanon into Israel by the Palestine Liberation Organisation (PLO) go as far back as 1968, following the Six-Day War. The area became a significant base for attacks with the arrival of the PLO leadership and its Fatah brigade following their 1971 expulsion from Jordan. Also, increasing demographic tensions related to the Lebanese National Pact began running high and led in part to the Lebanese Civil War.

Concurrently, Syria began a 29-year military occupation in 1976. Israel's 1978 invasion of Lebanon failed to stem the Palestinian attacks in the long run, but Israel invaded Lebanon again in 1982 and forcibly expelled the PLO. Israel withdrew to a borderland buffer zone in southern Lebanon, held with the aid of proxy militants in the South Lebanon Army (SLA).

Hezbollah's Foundation and Origins

In the early 1960s, Lebanon witnessed the beginning of a new clerical movement that served to reinvigorate Islam's key principles in clerical and political terms. The three leading Shia clerics were: Imam Mussa al-Sadr (who founded the "Movement of the Oppressed" as well as "The Ranks of Lebanese Resistance" (*Amal*), Sheikh Muhammad Mahdi Shamseddine (who dedicated most of his life to intellectual work as well as leading the Shia community) and Sayyed Muhammad Hussein Fadlallah, Hezbollah's spiritual guide. Each one of them had their own approach, practical logic and plan of action, but they all shared a belief in the necessity of taking action to change the prevalent condition of Lebanese Shiites. During the early years of Hezbollah, Sayyed Muhammad Hussein Fadlallah was a symbol of many ideological concepts within the Party, guiding Hezbollah through a mature vision of Islam and of the Islamic movement, and supporting Ayotollah Khomeini, the Islamic Revolution's leader in Iran. Even though he was considered as Hezbollah's spiritual leader, Sayyed Fadlallah always refused any participation in organised Hezbollah activity and opted to remain a cleric supporting those Party directives that he deemed harmonious with his views.

In 1979, the Iranian Revolution led by Ayatollah Ruhollah Khomeini, gave rise to political revitalisation in Lebanon. Ayatollah Khomeini was designated the leading religious authority within the Shiite community and the need to build a united Islamic organisation emerged. Thus, the representatives of the main Islamic groups began discussions about their perceptions of Islamic activity in Lebanon. These were summarised in a document, the "Manifesto of the Nine", which declared the following three objectives:

(1) Islam is the comprehensive, complete and appropriate programme for a better life;

(2) Resistance against Israeli occupation required a *jihad* (holy war);

(3) The legitimate leadership is that of the Jurist-Theologian (*wilayat al-faqih*) who is considered to be the successor to the Prophet and the Imams.

This document was presented to Ayatollah Khomeini, who granted his approval, thereby bestowing upon himself custodianship as Jurist-Theologian. Various Islamic groups then adopted the manifesto, dissolving their existing organisations in favour of this new framework, which came to be known as Hezbollah. All of these developments took place at a time of Iranian solidarity with Lebanon and Syria. Syria agreed to the passage of the Iranian Revolutionary Guard into Lebanon, and training camps were set up in the Western Bekaa Valley district.

Created following the 1982 Israeli invasion of Lebanon, Hezbollah became a major linchpin of the resistance against the occupation. The party's leadership succeeded, with Syrian and Iranian help, in creating a large network of institutions to answer the various social and humanitarian needs of the population of South Lebanon. In 1985, Hezbollah established itself politically and declared an armed struggle to end the Israeli occupation of Lebanese territory. When the Lebanese Civil War ended and other warring factions agreed to disarm, both Hezbollah and the SLA refused.

The Ta'if Accord

The Syrian regime never formally acknowledged Lebanon as a sovereign entity. There has been an absence of embassies representing the two countries in each other's capitals. In 1976, with US and Israeli support, President Hafez al-Assad of Syria sent his troops to Lebanon to maintain a state of controlled tension. Syria played Lebanese factions off against each other to maintain its supremacy. With Washington's tacit support, Syrian suzerainty over Lebanon lasted for thirty years.

The end of the civil war in Lebanon saw the country undergo a period of amazing reconstruction shepherded by Prime Minister Rafiq al-Hariri. With his contacts and global friendships, al-Hariri brought back to Lebanon a respect it had lost and a role it used to have. The major drawback was that he focused on physical reconstruction at the expense of reconciliation between the Lebanese.

Reconciliation between Lebanon's various communities never really occurred. The Christians in particular felt defeated and betrayed while the Sunnis and the Shias took more control of the instruments of power in the country. The other major fault line was Hezbollah's ever-increasing role and influence. Mostly dominated by Lebanese Shias, Hezbollah became the paramount military and social power in South Lebanon. Calls to send Lebanese troops to the border with Israel were always met with resistance.

The Ta'if Agreement (*ittifāqiyat al-Tā'if*) (National Reconciliation Accord) was an agreement reached to provide the basis for the ending of the civil war and the return to political normalcy in Lebanon. Negotiated in Ta'if, Saudi Arabia, it reasserted Lebanese authority in Southern Lebanon (then occupied by Israel). It also set a time frame for Syrian withdrawal in two years. It was signed on 22 October 1989 and ratified by the Lebanese parliament on 5 November 1989. The Agreement changed the ratio of Parliament to 1:1 and reduced the power of the Maronite president. Amendments made following the Lebanese Civil War transferred many presidential powers to a cabinet divided evenly between Christians and Muslims.

The Accord called for demilitarisation of all militias and withdrawal of all foreign forces. However, neither of these calls was fulfilled. On the contrary, the Accord itself underlined a strengthened role for Syria in Lebanese politics by empowering it to assist the Lebanese government in the implementation process and established a quasi-legal framework for Syrian dominance in Lebanese politics, especially in security and foreign policy issues, leading many to question Lebanon's sovereignty. Based on this agreement, the Syrians allowed Hezbollah's existence as an armed organisation under the pretext of continued confrontation with Israel.

The Syrian presence in Lebanon gave it important leverage over its own relations with Israel, in getting back the Golan Heights. General Michel Aoun, the Lebanese Army Commander, rebelled against this development. Lebanese army and Syrian troops took a decision to oust him through a military operation at the end of 1990.

Although militias of the civil war joined the central army, Hezbollah remained an exception and continued to keep its arms. The first elections of the post-civil war Lebanon were held in 1992, which Hezbollah entered as a political party winning eight seats, giving it the largest single bloc in the 128-member parliament. With an additional four seats of its allies, its power was further strengthened in the Parliament. As a political party, it gained a reputation for being 'clean' and 'uncorrupted', increasing its popularity.

Since the beginning of the Second Intifada (2001), Hamas and Hezbollah forged a close political and military alliance.The US invasion of Iraq in 2003 consolidated Iran as a major player in the region. The Shiite arc of influence now extended all the way from Tehran to Basra, to Beirut. Hezbollah became a convenient instrument for Iran's policies against US interests in the region.

Following the assassination of Lebanese Prime Minister Rafiq al-Hariri, in February 2005, UN Security Council Resolution (UNSCR) 1559 was adopted calling for the exit of all foreign troops from Lebanon (meaning

Syria) and the dismantling of Hezbollah as a militia. Prime Minister Hariri had always challenged Syria's pre-eminent role in Lebanon. He lobbied hard with his European and American friends to have the UN adopt the resolution. In the spring of 2005, following al-Hariri's assassination, Syria was forced to pull its troops out of the country. The rationale was that Israel had ended its occupation of South Lebanon and the Hezbollah resistance movement had become moot, but this was not Hezbollah's interpretation. For the Shia-dominated militia Israel was still in occupation of the Shab'a Farms (an area of around 20-25 square kilometres in South Lebanon) and this justified it keeping its weapons. (See Appendix A)

The Lebanese-Israeli Conflict

Because Israel and Lebanon have never signed a peace accord, the countries remain officially in a state of war that has existed since 1948 when Lebanon joined other Arab nations against the newly-formed Jewish state. The two countries have been bound by an armistice signed in 1949, which regulates the presence of military forces in southern Lebanon.

With a large Christian minority in an overwhelmingly Muslim region, mercantile and Westernised, Lebanon was considered the least hostile Arab neighbour to Israel—and the weakest. The rare skirmishes that occurred were mostly symbolic. That began to change when Palestinian guerrillas became active. In 1968, Israeli commandos landed at Beirut airport and blew up 13 Lebanese airliners in retaliation for Arab militants firing on an Israeli airliner in Athens, Greece.

Under pressure from staunch anti-Israeli Arab regimes in 1969, Lebanon signed an agreement that effectively gave away its southern region for Palestinian guerrillas to use as a springboard to infiltrate Israel or launch cross-border attacks. Notable among these were an April 1974 raid on the northern Israeli town of Kiryat Shmona, when Palestinian gunmen killed 16 civilians, mostly women and children, and an attack the following month on a school in Maalot in which a militant group killed 20 teenagers.

Israel retaliated regularly as Palestinian guerrillas fired on northern Israel, and Israeli forces invaded southern Lebanon in 1978. A UN peacekeeping force was deployed and the Israelis pulled out after installing a local Lebanese militia in the border buffer zone, but the attacks continued. Israel invaded again, on a larger scale, in 1982 to destroy Yasser Arafat's PLO movement, which had established itself as a force within Lebanon during the country's civil war that began in 1975. The bulk of Palestinian guerrillas were evacuated from Lebanon, but Hezbollah emerged with the aid of Iran. US-sponsored negotiations produced a Lebanon-Israel agreement which collapsed as Lebanon lapsed in another round of civil war. After a destructive and costly military campaign that lasted for three years, Israeli forces withdrew from most of Lebanon but retained a self-proclaimed "security zone" just north of its own border.

The IDF's 1982 invasion of Lebanon, named Operation ***Peace for Galilee***, was designed to destroy the PLO threat to Israel and shatter its capacity to wage war. At the onset of the campaign, three Israeli army divisions rapidly moved north to the outskirts of Beirut, trapping and killing numerous PLO members and driving the remnants into headlong retreat. At the same time, the Israeli Air Force (IAF) destroyed most of the Syrian air defence systems in Lebanon without any loss. Although the IDF defeated the PLO, it still faced a large Lebanese population who were not happy with the Israeli occupation. Initially greeted as liberators the IDF became seen as occupiers.

Plagued by unremitting attacks spearheaded by Hezbollah and other secular groups, the IDF withdrew into southern Lebanon in 1985. In the new security zone, which encompassed 10 percent of Lebanon, the IDF and its ally, the SLA, began constructing a string of company-size fortified outposts. Ignoring United Nations Resolution 425, which called for a complete Israeli withdrawal from Lebanon, the IDF and SLA prepared for a lengthy stay. Israel made it clear that, unless they could have some assurance against terrorist border incursions and rocket attacks from Lebanon, they would remain in the security zone.

Hezbollah, however, was determined to drive the IDF out of Lebanon, believing that, unless attacks continued, the Israelis would never leave. Beginning in 1985, they relentlessly assaulted the IDF and SLA in the security zone. Hezbollah developed 13 principles of war, specifically designed to defeat a relatively fixed, technologically advanced enemy.

1. Avoid the strong, attack the weak—attack and withdrawal.
2. Protecting our fighters is more important than causing enemy casualties.
3. Strike only when success is assured.
4. Surprise is essential to success. If you are spotted, you have failed.

5. Don't get into a set-piece battle. Slip away like smoke, before the enemy can drive home his advantage.
6. Attaining the goal demands patience, in order to discover the enemy's weak points.
7. Keep moving; avoid formation of a front line.
8. Keep the enemy on constant alert, at the front and in the rear.
9. The road to the great victory passes through thousands of small victories.
10. Keep up the morale of the fighters; avoid notions of the enemy's superiority.
11. The media has innumerable guns whose hits are like bullets. Use them in the battle.
12. The population is a treasure—nurture it.
13. Hurt the enemy and then stop before he abandons restraint.

Hezbollah's doctrine helped accomplish a number of goals, two of which included:

1. Confusing the enemy and obliging its command to call for a constant state of alert, eventually leading to exhaustion and decline in power.
2. Spreading panic among enemy troops, the fear of death persisted after every successful or possible resistance attack. This served to shake enemy morale and subsequently affected troop performance.

The doctrine provided an exceptionally effective blueprint for victory. By the 1990s, Hezbollah had transformed itself into a highly competent resistance organisation, as well as a political party with extensive support among the Lebanese population. Its principal intent was to make the Israelis and the SLA have as costly a withdrawal as possible by imposing casualties that further eroded the troops' morale and increased domestic pressure for their departure. A constant stream of casualties on Israeli military forces through suicide bombings, sophisticated ambushes, and direct attacks on the IDF and SLA were often captured on film and shown on Hezbollah's television station, *al-Manar*. The disturbing images were also beamed into Israeli households, depicting the horrors of war often muted by Israeli television.

The Israelis did not remain entirely on the defensive. In 1993, in response to increased casualties in the security zone, they launched Operation ***Accountability***. Hezbollah had prepared for an Israeli ground offensive but was taken aback by the massive Israeli air and artillery campaign waged against them. The military operation was unlike any Hezbollah had encountered as the Israelis chiefly employed standoff-based precision firepower. It proved a valuable lesson and one that would better prepare Hezbollah for the next war.

The next major clash between Hezbollah and Israel came in 1996. When Hezbollah rockets wounded 38 civilians in northern Israel, the IDF unleashed Operation ***Grapes of Wrath***. Once again, the IDF generally resorted to standoff-based precision firepower. The IDF campaign targeted not only Hezbollah but also civilian infrastructure and civilian population centres in southern Lebanon. Israel expected to cause a mass exodus of civilians from southern Lebanon, forcing the Lebanese and Syrian governments to take action against Hezbollah. The operation was designed to force the hand of the Lebanese and Syrian governments and not to destroy Hezbollah's military capabilities. Not surprisingly, Operation ***Grapes of Wrath*** failed and served only to further alienate scores of Lebanese people and produce widespread international scorn.

As Israeli precision-guided weapons and bombs rained down on southern Lebanon, Hezbollah struck back at northern Israel with hundreds of Katyusha rockets, forcing thousands of Israelis to seek cover in bomb shelters. The Hezbollah Secretary-General, Hassan Nasrallah, made it clear that if Israel hits Lebanese civilian targets, then Hezbollah would retaliate. Although Israel inflicted heavy losses on Hezbollah, at no time during Operation ***Grapes of Wrath*** was the IDF's standoff precision weaponry able to silence Hezbollah's rockets. It was a lesson noted by Hezbollah and entirely ignored by the IDF. With Hezbollah capable of responding in kind, both sides reached a tacit agreement, on 26 April 1996, not to target civilians.

On 28 February 1999, a small Israeli convoy of vehicles was ambushed near the village of Kafr Shaba, in the Israeli-occupied security zone of south Lebanon. In the convoy was Brigadier General Erez Gerstein, commander of the IDF in southern Lebanon, a legendary figure. Gerstein was killed along with two others. The killing of the highest-ranking Israeli officer in Lebanon by Hezbollah confirmed its status as Israel's most intractable enemy. The ambush was filmed by Hezbollah and aired on all Lebanese television stations. While Gerstein's death had little effect militarily, it was nonetheless a psychological defeat for Israelis. By March 1999, a majority of Israelis were demanding an end to the Lebanese quagmire. For over 20 years, Israel had waged an almost continual military campaign in Lebanon, first in opposition to the PLO, then against a variety of Lebanese groups determined to force the Israelis out of their country.

As the war in southern Lebanon continued, mounting IDF casualties propelled anti-war groups into the political spotlight as politicians and a preponderance of the public called for a unilateral withdrawal from Lebanon. The strength of the anti-war movement compelled Ehud Barak, a candidate for Prime Minister at the time, to promise a withdrawal from Lebanon if elected. Upon his election in 1999, Barak assured the Israelis he would remove the IDF from southern Lebanon within 12 months, either bilaterally or unilaterally.

Hezbollah, however, was determined to accelerate the Israeli withdrawal. It offered leniency to all SLA members who surrendered before the withdrawal began, while continuing its attacks on SLA and IDF outposts in the security zone. New SLA defections to Hezbollah greatly alarmed the Israelis. When the IDF shut down four forward outposts near the town of Jezzine in June 1999, SLA units began withdrawing from their outposts within the city limits. Hezbollah fighters quickly moved into the town and continued to pummel the dwindling ranks of the SLA as they moved into new positions to the south.

Israeli Withdrawal in 2000

In January 2000, the SLA was badly shaken by the assassination of one of its key leaders. Aql Hashim was killed when Hezbollah managed to place a bomb inside his house. Once again, SLA defections picked up pace. When discussions in Geneva between Syria, Israel, and the US fell apart, in March 2000, Barak announced that by July 2000, the army will withdraw to the international border.

After Barak's announcement, the Israeli government assured the SLA they would be protected and promised them sanctuary in Israel. However, the word never filtered down to the ranks, which left them discouraged and dispirited. On 21 May 2000, SLA soldiers abandoned their positions in the town of Taibe. By the end of the day, an SLA Shiite brigade in the central sector of the security zone collapsed, with scores of soldiers surrendering to Hezbollah.

On 22 May, the IDF ordered all SLA intelligence officials to withdraw from the security zone and move to the Israeli border. As other SLA units pulled back, they destroyed their bunkers and outposts. By the end of the day, it was readily apparent that the IDF was accelerating its withdrawal.

By 23 May, the SLA had completely disintegrated. Its western brigade at Bint Jbeil was ordered to pull back to the Israeli border, while the Druze brigade in the east simply melted away. In many cases, the IDF and the SLA abandoned their military equipment. When the infamous SLA prison at Khiam was liberated that afternoon, Hezbollah's *al-Manar* broadcast the event live around the world. At the border, chaos reigned as IDF and SLA forces retreated into Israel, telling reporters that their military equipment and training had proven useless against Hezbollah, and its Lebanese allies.

As each outpost fell, Hezbollah planted its yellow flags atop the fortifications. Israeli citizens along the border watched, only a short distance from their settlements. Along the border fence, crowds gathered to taunt and throw stones at the Israeli soldiers manning observation towers on the other side. The Israeli withdrawal from the security zone was seen as a complete fiasco. One Israeli newspaper called the last day of the withdrawal a "Day of Humiliation". Israel was defeated by Hezbollah in Lebanon, forcing its withdrawal on 24 May 2000. Ultimately, the fighting qualities of Hezbollah, Israeli war fatigue, and uncertain allies turned the withdrawal into an embarrassing rout. The withdrawal of the IDF, in May 2000, also led to the collapse of the SLA. A second round was inevitable.

Hezbollah quickly took control of the area. Later, citing continued Israeli control of the Shab'a farms and the internment of Lebanese prisoners in Israel, Hezbollah intensified its cross-border attacks, and used the tactic of seizing soldiers from Israel as leverage for a prisoner exchange. From 2000, after the Israeli withdrawal, till 2006, Hezbollah conducted approximately 200 attacks on Israel—most of them artillery fire, some raids and some via proxies inside Israel. In these attacks, including the attack that precipitated the Israeli response that developed into the war, 31 Israelis were killed and 104 were wounded.

Israel withdrew from Lebanon in 2000 without coordinating the conditions for evacuating the security zone in South Lebanon with the

Lebanese government. However, it did coordinate its withdrawal with the United Nations: representatives of the UN secretary general drew the so-called Blue Line as the demarcation line between Israel and Lebanon (the agreement of both nations would have been necessary to establish a permanent border). On this basis, the UN approved the declaration that Israel was withdrawing from all of Lebanon, except for the northern part of the village of Ghajar.

Hezbollah exploited the IDF's hasty exit and the subsequent vacuum in southern Lebanon. It cultivated a narrative of victory, by the fact that Israel had failed to confront the organisation's resistance (*mukawamah*) successfully. It seized control of the areas evacuated by Israel, entrenching the organisation and making the organisation into the de facto ruler, while continuing acts of provocation against Israel. Hezbollah also strengthened its influence on the Lebanese political system, including participation in elections and the government. On the military level, the organisation built its military strength with Syrian and Iranian support, with surface-to-surface missiles and rockets, advanced and portable anti-tank and anti-air missile systems, UAVs for intelligence gathering and attacks, and surface-to-sea missiles. It constructed underground infrastructures for launches, concealment tunnels, and intelligence and command and control systems. Hezbollah reorganised its strategic model, basing its efforts on the firepower capabilities of a regular army combined with a modus operandi of guerrilla warfare, and reorganised its command and control structure. Finally, it provided direct and indirect help to Palestinian terrorist organisations in planning, financing, and arming terrorist attacks.

The Syrian Withdrawal from Lebanon

After the Israeli withdrawal, some political groups began to call for a Syrian withdrawal from Lebanon, to contribute to Lebanon's 'normalisation' and restoration of its sovereignty. Despite these calls, Syria continued its presence in the country and maintained close ties especially with Shi'a groups and Hezbollah. However, after the US invasion of Iraq in 2003, the Syrian presence in Lebanon came under scrutiny once again.

The US administration increased its pressure on Syria with a regime change discourse. On 11 May 2004, President Bush approved the decision of the Senate that called for imposing sanctions on Syria. UNSCR 1559 of September 2004, called for the "disbanding and disarming of Lebanese and non-Lebanese militias, the extension of the control of the government of Lebanon over all its territory, the strict respect of the sovereignty, territorial integrity, unity and political independence of Lebanon, and fair and free presidential elections according to the Lebanese constitutional rules without foreign interference and influence. The assassination of the former Prime Minister Rafiq Hariri on 14 February 2005 brought the Lebanese politics yet to another juncture.

The groups that gathered in the Martyr's Square on 14 March to protest the Hariri assassination, later known as the 14 March Forces, brought together different groups that were against the Syrian presence in the country. This movement was called the Cedar Revolution. Under pressure, Syria withdrew its military and intelligence services from Lebanon on 27 April 2005. The May 2005 general elections were the first elections without a Syrian military presence in Lebanon after decades. Two main groups, the 14 March and the 8 March, competed in the election. The 14 March group won 72 seats, while the pro-Syrian coalition won 56 seats in Parliament. The Lebanese political system was thus deeply divided.

This was the background to the events of 12 July 2006, when Hezbollah launched a surprise attack on an IDF patrol along the Lebanese border inside Israeli territory, abducted two soldiers, murdered three, and injured three others. The abduction, less than three weeks after an IDF soldier, Gilad Shalit, was abducted along Israel's border with the Gaza Strip, was assisted by surface-to-surface missile fire toward northern Israel. Hezbollah leader Hassan Nasrallah assumed Israel's reaction would be mild, given that the IDF's attention was focused on the Gaza Strip, that there had been no significant Israeli response to the 2000 abductions or the attempted abductions in 2005-2006. This assumption was likewise grounded in Hezbollah's, as well as Nasrallah's own, self-confidence in an ability to predict Israeli reactions to any event.

GEOGRAPHIC AND TERRAIN ANALYSIS

Historical Background

The story of the border between Lebanon and Israel, delineated between French Syria and British Palestine between 1916 and 1923 is regarded as one of the strangest enigmas of modern times. It is the result of high-handed colonial politics undertaken in ignorance of the realities on the ground.

During the First World War, when it became evident that the Ottoman Empire was being defeated, the then world powers, France and Britain discussed future plans to share the spoils in the Middle East. France, which had historic ties with the Maronite Catholic community in the Levant focused its attention on northern territories in Lebanon and Syria, while Great Britain sought contacts with the Arabs due to the recently discovered oil in the Persian Gulf. There were also other groups interested in Palestine, apart from the Arabs—the Jewish Zionists, who had been promised a national home in Palestine in 1917, by the then British Foreign Secretary Arthur James Balfour. But the roots of the Lebanon-Israel border lie in the May 1916 Sykes-Picot Agreement, the outcome of secret negotiations between Sir Mark Sykes, MP and the French Arabist, François Georges Picot, former consul general in Beirut. The spheres of influence created by the agreement would have left the watersheds in the region divided in a particularly convoluted manner: the Litani (otherwise known as Quasimiya) river and the Jordan headwaters would be under French control, while the Sea of Galilee would be divided between Britain and France. The reasons for this oversight were the strategic locations of railway and oil lines, which British negotiators at the time viewed as of utmost importance to their imperial strategy. Water resources were regarded as of marginal importance in the border demarcation process.

In December 1918, following the conquest of Palestine and Syria, the British Government no longer felt obligated to defer to French political interests and, during preliminary negotiations on the delineation of the boundaries, signalled a more determined attitude. The British were also prepared to consider Zionist requests in a more positive way. The British deviated from the Sykes-Picot line and adopted the Biblical concept for Palestine, as based on an ancient map. The French did not agree. In the ongoing negotiations over the temporary boundaries of the occupied lands, the British persisted in their demand to stretch the northern border line of Palestine up to the Litani River and across to the Banias springs on the slopes of Mount Hermon which was welcomed by the Zionists, who regarded their water requirements as a vital issue.

The British negotiators, mostly military veterans of World War I, considered Britain's strategy from a purely security point of view. To them, the Litani gorge presented the only natural border between Palestine and Lebanon. It is unfortunate, in view of subsequent events, that this viewpoint with its far-reaching strategic implications was a casualty of lengthy political haggling and was ignored. The resultant 'impossible' geopolitical situation has haunted Middle Eastern politics ever since.

During the 1919 Paris Peace Conference, the Arab delegation headed by Emir Feisal of Hejaz actually supported the Jewish demands in Palestine and tried to assist Zionist leader Chaim Weizman's position against the French policies in Lebanon. During the discussions, the two parties agreed that all water and boundary issues should be settled through direct bilateral negotiations, the only time that such a proposal was officially aired by an Arab leader. It could have become an important turning point, but short-sighted colonial considerations soon rendered this proposal null and void.

At the Versailles conference, in February 1919, the final decisions over the demarcation of the Palestine-Lebanese border were left to British and French negotiators. The French supported the Lebanese claim that the "*historical and natural*" boundaries of "*Greater Lebanon*" should include the sources of the Jordan River. This was totally unacceptable to the British and in 1919 they suggested the so-called *Meinertzhagen Line* as a compromise, which fulfilled most of Britain's security requirements. This line was similar to the Zionist proposal and was rejected by the French, for that very reason. Then followed another British proposal, a compromise called the *1919 Deauville Proposal* which granted Palestine less territory than the Zionists demanded, but still included the southern bank of the Litani, which at least retained in place the natural obstacle for security. As the French negotiators hesitated and were about to reject that proposal as well, the British proposed a border line running from Acre, on the Mediterranean coast to the Litani river bend and then east to Mount Hermon, which would increase Lebanese territory, but still maintain the Litani gorge as a buffer zone. Although the French rejected each of these proposals and insisted on the original Sykes-Picot line, they did agree to some concessions, especially on the issue of the Jordan headwaters.

In June 1920 the French negotiators finally presented their own proposal: Palestine's northern border should run from Ras en-Naqoura to a point near the Jordan River just north of the Jewish settlement of Metulla and some nearby villages. The French remained adamant against last minute appeals, both British and Zionist, to include the Litani river. In December 1920, a final agreement was reached on the border issue, which mainly addressed French and British rail and oil interests, but totally ignored any topographical requirements for a feasible border line which could be defended through natural obstacles, or secure vital water resources for British Palestine (and later any Jewish Homeland).

The final boundary between the French and British mandates, which later became the border between Lebanon and Israel, was worked out by a joint Anglo-French commission set up to trace the final border demarcation on the ground. That was the intention but, unfortunately, it never materialised and the line agreed upon was never demarcated on the ground. The primary considerations, which determined the outcome of the compromise, were based on the wishes of the local inhabitants, who lived in the border region, mainly the Lebanese Shi'ites, and to a lesser extent, the few isolated Jewish settlements in the Jordan rift valley sloping uphill towards the western mountain ridge.

The commission, consisting of two officers, the French Lieutenant Colonel M. Paulet and British Lieutenant Colonel Stuart Newcombe, submitted its report, in February 1922, which was signed by their respective governments a year later, in March 1923. The result proved disastrous for future generations. Today's problems stem mainly from two major problems, which were overlooked at the time. The two officers decided to choose distinct physical landmarks to determine temporary ground features along the line traced by them on their maps. Yet many of these features were stones, trees and ancient foundations, which over the years disappeared completely, or shifted with the heavy winter flow of rivers and *wadis*. What proved even more confusing was the fact that the border delineation was conducted on 1:100,000 scale military maps which did not match, due to different techniques; the British using the standard topographical contours, and the French using their own shaded maps, which indicate the ground contours in visible terms. These were not always accurate at the time, lacking as they did modern survey technologies.

The inevitable result was that important tactical topographical features were ignored or failed completely to register during the demarcation, a failure which has direct bearing on the present problems being experienced in defining a line which can be accepted by both sides.

The Border Becomes a Battleground

From the start, the 1923 borderline existed only in theory. In practice it almost did not exist, at least for the inhabitants, both Jews and Arabs living in the *Galilee Panhandle* (a four-kilometre narrow strip of valley land protruding like a finger from the Hula valley northwards to Metulla, on the border with Lebanon. It is one of the strangest geopolitical phenomena, and has caused serious ethnic, political tensions ever since, mainly due to Israel's strategic insecurity of its northern border region, as well as the Lebanese Christians and Muslims living on the other side, who virtually ignored the line and went about their daily business, crossing into each other's territory unheeded. Travel and commerce continued throughout as before. In fact, removed from the political centre in Beirut, the mostly Shi'ite South was neglected by the central Lebanese administration, and thus remained a virtual economic extension of northern Palestine, in spite of the new border.

The result was twofold: on the one hand, the traditionally good neighbourly relations between Jews, Christians and Shi'ite Muslims remained close, but on the other, the lack of governmental control produced a haven for irresponsible elements, such as smugglers and armed Arab bands infiltrating into Palestine. It was a dangerous vacuum, and the situation grew substantially worse as the tension between Jews, Arabs and the British authorities finally erupted during the 1936-39 Arab Revolt. Arab irregulars, backed by Muslim radicals, used South Lebanon as a staging area for recruitment and training, and cross-border attacks became a daily routine. For the British authorities in Palestine, the northern border region became a prime strategic focal point and urgent measures to counter the dangerous infiltration routes had to be taken if Northern Palestine was to remain under firm military control. It was here, for the first time, that the British military commanders realised how erratically their predecessors had negotiated the border demarcation. The British Army in Palestine was the first to pay the price for this political negligence. It became strikingly obvious that while the negotiators in the 1920s had concentrated mainly on economic, strategic and religious interests, they had almost totally neglected security issues, an approach which was now about to backfire with serious consequences.

A significant event, during the riots of 1938, was the arrival in Palestine of Sir Charles Tegart who had been sent to advise on counter terrorist activities. Tegart immediately set about reconnoitring the borderline and his first report was straight to the point: it could not, from a military viewpoint be defended along most of its length, under the prevailing topographical conditions.

In an attempt to seal off the border against incursions from Lebanon the construction of a frontier road, with barbed wire fences along the entire length was authorised. Further, a number of concrete blockhouses were built at vantage points, at prescribed intervals along the fence. But it was of little use. With the topographic disadvantage of so many potential flash points remaining unchanged, the infiltrators had little difficulty in overcoming the fence, circumventing the manned pillboxes, as well as evading the mobile patrols along the frontier road, which was usually under full observation from vantage points inside the Lebanese border region.

During World War II, the Palestine-Lebanese border region was the site of further conflict, when the British Army invaded Vichy-French controlled Lebanon and Syria. Throughout the war, there were several fights in the border area and it was again evident that the border was strategically unsound and difficult to defend. Lebanon was granted independence in 1944 (Syria in 1946) and the border officially closed down again. Also during this period there were some initiatives that, if brought to fruition, could have possibly reversed some of the worst effects of the colonial legacy and contributed to peace in the area. One such plan was the ambitious project to harness the Litani River for hydroelectric power through a joint Lebanese-Palestinian-Jewish company, funded by American Jews. But the French authorities opposed such a move and the plans were discarded. An opportunity was lost, which could have dramatically repaired one of the drastic colonial mistakes, which had created the difficult problems in the border region.

The Arab-Israeli Wars on Lebanon's Frontier

Although the small Lebanese army did not play a significant role during the 1948 Arab-Israeli War, it nevertheless attacked and captured two small Israeli villages along the international border. During Operation *Hiram* in October 1948, the Israelis counter-attacked and gained control over the entire Lebanese border region, capturing 14 Lebanese villages and reaching the banks of the Litani, for the first time. Here once again opportunity presented itself, when some of the Christian and Shi'ite village heads approached the Israeli commanders and asked for their protection against the Sunni Muslim marauders who had for years maltreated them. The Israeli authorities refused, and when the Israeli forces withdrew under the 1949 armistice agreement, the entire matter was shelved. The missed opportunities turned the border into a battlefield.

The March 1949 Armistice Agreement between Israel and Lebanon produced no controversy, except for a small stretch of border in the eastern sector. In general, the old 1923 borderline was reinstated and remained intact, in relative peace, even during the 1967 war. However, following the eviction of the PLO guerrillas from Jordan in September 1970, the PLO established its base in South Lebanon, filling the vacuum that existed there. They then exploited the chaotic situation that prevailed in Lebanon following the civil war in1976. The border, and especially its northern and eastern sectors, again turned into zone of conflict as Palestinian guerrillas carried out deadly cross-border raids into northern Israel, which culminated in a major confrontation in 1978, as Israel retaliated by force with Operation *Litani.* Because the fighting did not subside, the Israelis struck again in 1982, this time reaching Beirut and forcing the PLO to leave Lebanon.

Eventually, the IDF withdrew from Lebanon in 1985 and another opportunity to form some sort of a peaceful coexistence with the Shi'ite population was lost, when the moderate Shi'ite Amal party approached the IDF for assistance in their struggle against the newly created radical

Map 1: Israeli–Lebanon Border, 1949-1967

Shi'ite Hezbollah. Due to short sighted Israeli policies, which still favoured the Maronite Christians in the north, rather than throw in their lot with the Shi'ite neighbours who were the real co-habitants of the border region, this was refused. Years later, when the Iran-backed Hezbollah fighters fought a fierce guerrilla war against the IDF in the Israeli-established Security Zone in South Lebanon, the Israelis were to regret this and would pay dearly for these short sighted mistakes until finally forced to withdraw under extremely inopportune circumstances in May 2000.

Description of the Israel-Lebanon Boundary

The international boundary, ratified by Great Britain and France in 1923, is about 120 kilometres in length. It can be divided into four different topographical segments:

Sector A—stretches from Ras-en Naqoura to Sarit, about 15 kilometres in length;

Sector B—traces a twisted line along about twice that length from Sarit to Malqiye;

Sector C—runs along the high ground from Malqiye to Metulla; and,

Sector D—is the eastern segment, stretching from Metulla to the Syrian border.

Sector A. Leaves the Mediterranean coast at the cliffs of Ras en Naqoura and follows the crest of the spur towards Hanita, then running southwards it follows the *thalweg* (a principle, traditionally applied to river boundaries, referring to a division along the deepest part of the deepest navigable channel) of Wadi Qutaya, a deep crevasse-like gorge. It then runs up the *thalweg* of a small tributary, turns into Wadi Idlam and then circumventing an area of high ground to the south, follows the *thalweg* of Wadi e-Dalib. Up to this point, the borderline offers good defensive positions and little advantage to infiltrators from the north. However, in the stretch that follows up to the Sarit settlement, which is located right next to the international borderline, the ground on Israel's side is nearly impossible to defend.On the Lebanese side of the border there are several 700-metre high hills, which dominate the entire length of the Israeli border road, and place the Jewish settlements under constant threat from small arms fire. Here, the IDF maintained its security zone, constructing outposts to control the area from well-placed observation sites.

Sector B. This is one of the more dangerous segments of the border, with no natural obstacles at all and most of the Israeli border section is under full hostile observation. Except for the cover offered by a few 600-700-metre crests, which are bisected by the international boundary, the Jewish border settlements of Shetula, Dovev, Baram and especially Avivim, which is directly along the border line, are all vulnerable to hostile fire from vantage positions in Lebanese territory. What are even more dangerous are the *wadis* running in a southerly direction and offering excellent infiltration routes.

Sector C. Here the border starts in the valley overlooked by Jebel a-Dere inside Lebanon. Thence it follows the *thalweg* in a generally northern direction. It then climbs to the narrow 700-metre-plus ridge, which separates the Galilee Panhandle from the Golan Heights to the east. Along most of this stretch the border roads on the Israeli and Lebanese side, run less than 100 metres from each other, with the road on the Israeli side actually hugging the border line itself in several places. The Israeli Kibutz Manara is located directly on the border, dominated by an 800-metre high hill. As the eastern ridge is less than a few hundred metres wide and falls steeply downhill into the Jordan Valley, Manara is highly vulnerable to hostile fire on its sole approach road from the north. A few kilometres north, the mountain village of Margaliot is dominated by two Lebanese hills, the 780-metre Tel a Tsebih and the 820-metre Tel e-Qaba. To the south is Tel Sheikh Abed, which houses a Jewish and Muslim holy site, which is now bisected right through its middle by the international border, a most sensitive point for those visiting the site. The line follows the ridge northward, to Kibutz Misgav Am, located near the border line, a stone's throw from the Lebanese village of Odeisse and finally reaches Metulla the most northern village located at the tip of the Galilee pan-handle.

Sector D. The last section, delineated in the 1923 Anglo-French agreement, turns sharply to the southeast and originally followed the ancient path from Metulla to Banias. About 4 kilometres eastward it reaches the old Roman bridge over the River Hasbani. Here, near Jisr al Ghajar, was the location of the tri-border point between Lebanon, Syria and Israel, before the 1967 Six Day War. From there to the western slopes of Mount Hermon now stretches the sole remaining disputed area between Israel and Lebanon, the Sha'ba Farms which could become a flash point in the future, if the matter cannot be resolved by peaceful negotiation.

Current Controversial Border Issues

The Israeli Army withdrew from its security zone in South Lebanon in May 2000, in compliance with UN Resolution 425. The speed of the withdrawal, without the agreement of the UN or Lebanon took the UNIFIL by surprise. The UN swiftly announced that it intended to mark the international border and confirm that Israel had completely withdrawn before deploying peacekeepers along the border. The UN confirmed by 30 May that Israel and the Lebanese militia, the SLA, had left the interior of Lebanon, but the confirmation of the withdrawal to the internationally recognised border awaited the results of UN technical teams surveying and marking the line of the border. However, although UN Resolution 425 (1978) called on Israel to pull back to Lebanon's "*internationally recognised boundaries*", by May 2000 no one could agree any more on where the boundary lay. The UN therefore decided on a blue "*withdrawal line*" where it thought the border should run, to allow it to certify Israel's compliance with the resolution. The UN insists that the Blue Line is only temporary and it does not affect any future boundary demarcation, but the Lebanese government was reluctant to accept this compromise and raised many objections to the line of the border and claimed many "*violations*" of the border by Israel.

Following the 1982 War, when the IDF withdrew from Lebanon for the first time, Israel built a sophisticated defence complex along the border, consisting of electrified fences, anti-personal minefields, patrol roads and barbed wire obstacles. Because of the problematic nature of the topography, and the need to adjust to changes due to erosion and floods, the fence did not follow the precise 1923 /49 borderline. The new line was designated the "*Purple Line*" by the IDF on their military maps.

As a result, on some parts of the border, the 1982 security system protruded into Lebanese territory, in others it retreated into Israel. Most of these deviations have now been rectified through the UN topographical survey commission, which worked with the Lebanese and Israeli authorities in delineating the "*old*" international border, to be called the "*UN Blue Line.*"

At present, more than half of the 120-kilometre borderline is not delineated in any formal agreement between Israel and Lebanon. Topographical constraints leave the IDF vulnerable in their new locations along the UN designated "*Blue Line*", and the situation is further aggravated by the deployment close to the international border of Hezbollah strong points, from which they can reopen hostilities on Israeli military and civilian positions close to the border line.

The UN Blue Line differs from the 1949 Armistice Demarcation Line in three places: South of Remeishe, between Odeisse and Kibbutz Misgav Am and at Jisr Hasbani in the east. In fact, the situation became so absurd, that according to the UN cartographic team charged with defining the exact locations of the border, it would run through the centre of Kibutz Misgav with about half ending up in Lebanon. A compromise was finally reached under which the Blue Line would be shifted some 200 metres westward so that the border now brushes the western edge of the *kibbutz*, then drops downhill to the Odeisse road then follows the southern side of Kfar Kila and Metulla.

The other area, which remains under dispute, is even more bizarre. It concerns the Alawite village of Al-Ghajar, 4km east of Metulla. The UN cartographers, under Miklos Pinther, produced one of the strangest controversies during the already very complicated delineation process. Al-Ghajar, is located on the Hasbani river alongside the Wazzani springs, an important perennial source of the river. British military maps in 1940 erroneously placed the village in Lebanon, then still under French Mandate. At the time the matter was unimportant. The Israeli Army carried the error into their own maps, and during the capture of the Golan Heights, in 1967, avoided entering the village. The residents, regarded themselves as Syrian citizens and asked the Israelis to occupy the village. In the following years, the village flourished and grew to the north, absorbing the Lebanese hamlet of Al- Wazzani. When the UN surveyors started to probe into this area, they depicted Al- Ghajar as two thirds inside Lebanon and the other third within Israeli-occupied Syria, creating a security problem. The fate of Al-Ghajar is yet to be decided.

The last major controversy between Israel and Lebanon is the Har Dov sector, on the foothills of Mount Hermon concerns the Sha'ba Farms. A detailed description of this problem is at Appendix A.

Terrain Analysis

Comprising a rough rectangle, some 100 kilometres north to south and 75 kilometres east to west, southern Lebanon is compartmentalised in both directions. Several key rivers flow into the sea from the east and form

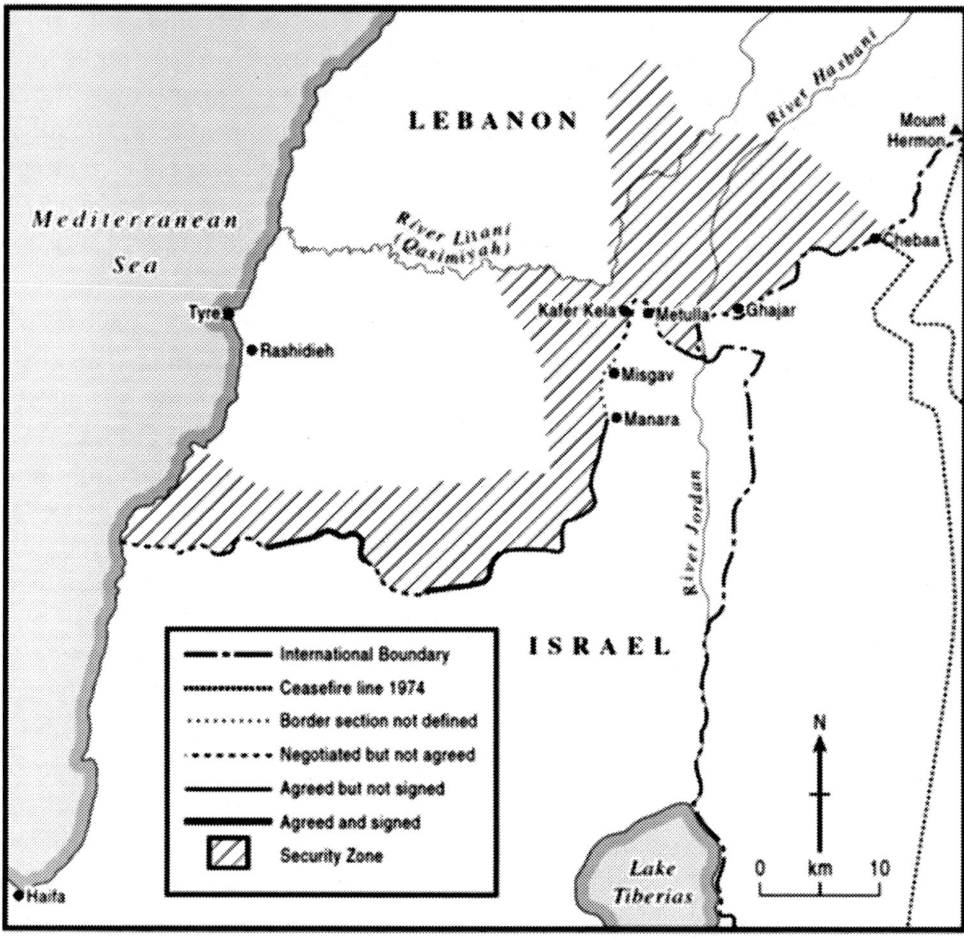

Map 2: Israel–Lebanon Border Enigma

potential barriers: the Litani, north of Tyre; the Zaharani, eight kilometres south of Sidon; the Awali, just north of Sidon; and the Damour, 14 kilometres south of Beirut. The major terrain zones, however, run north-south: the coastal plain, which extends anywhere from a few metres to several kilometres from the Mediterranean to the foothills of the mountains; the Lebanon ridge, which ranges from foothills to heights of 1,800 meters, encompasses the Shouf and Jbaal Barouk subranges, and covers roughly two-thirds of the area of southern Lebanon; the Bekaa Valley, a flat but narrow plain beginning some 25 kilometres north of the Israeli border and extending into northern Lebanon; and the Anti-Lebanon Ridge, which forms a natural border between Lebanon and Syria from Mount Hermon in the south to the Beirut-Damascus highway.

In tactical terms, the terrain is ideally suited to the defence, especially against armour. In all zones the roads are few, narrow, and poor. In the coastal zone, the main road is bordered by the sea and the hills, and when the plain does widen somewhat, citrus groves cover the area. Few parallel tracks exist, and *wadis* and ravines inhibit off-road movement. Along the road itself, the rivers form obstacles, and the towns of Tyre, Sidon, and Damour are build astride the road. On the Lebanon ridge, the roads are worse, steep and serpentine, with villages at every level area, hilltop, and crossroads; in the Jbaal Barouk area, only one north-south road exists, with numerous turns overlooked by steep cliffs. In the Bekaa, the valley floor does have several roads and allows for off-road movement, but the entire valley can be covered by direct-fire weapons from the bordering hills; in addition, the lower Lebanon ridge must be crossed in order even to reach the Bekaa. The Anti-Lebanon is virtually impassable, with almost no road: and numerous steep *wadis*. The overall effect of the terrain on tactical formations is to slow and channelise motorised movement, reducing a formation's combat strength to that of its lead element.

From a military standpoint, the terrain in South Lebanon seems totally unsuited for armoured warfare. It favours the defender, with its rugged, hilly countryside. Rock-covered basalt hills with steep ravines make cross-country movement, even with tanks, extremely difficult, and in most cases armoured vehicles are road- or track-bound. As the ridges normally run from east to west, movement is geared through the *wadis*, between the ridges. These are passable only in part and, with their steep canyon—like walls, make formidable obstacles.

Most of the region has thick shrubs, providing excellent hiding places for tank-hunter teams and ambushes that are very difficult to detect before they are executed. Furthermore, the area is filled with hundreds of small villages, mostly situated on the high ground, from which guerrilla fighters can mount their surprise attacks and swiftly return to good hiding places amongst the mostly friendly local Shiite population.

The Israeli deployment in the so-called Security Zone in South Lebanon is implemented through a series of strongpoints located widely apart and not always capable of rendering mutual fire support. One of the most difficult tasks is to maintain lines of communications to and from those strongpoints and the supply depots on the Israeli border. As most of the roads are winding narrow tracks, they provide the attackers with easy access to ambush sites, where they emplace explosive charges and mount rocket attacks on IDF traffic. Most of the costly IDF losses have been caused by such ambushes, and considerable effort is necessary in order to maintain open supply routes to the strongpoints. This is one of armour's major tasks in this continuous war.

The importance of terrain, even in this period of modern warfare, was again demonstrated in the fighting in the south. Israel would fight Hezbollah on intricate physical terrain that Hezbollah understood and had organised in a sophisticated way for defence.

The terrain of southern Lebanon offers decided advantages to the defender. It consists of both lowlands and highlands, and stark variations in climate, soil type, and vegetation occur across short distances. Tyre is the only major city in the region, and many of the villages, where most of the predominantly Shia population live, are located on top of small hills separated by deep valleys. The nature of the landscape restricts and channelises armoured manoeuvre and forces wheeled vehicles to remain on easily identifiable and exposed roads that are ideal sites for ambushes and for the employment of mines and IEDs. The terrain demands well-trained infantry and integrated fire and manoeuvre. Although armoured forces (tanks and armoured personnel carriers) faced mobility challenges in the terrain of southern Lebanon, they can, if employed properly, provide vital protected mobility and firepower. For the defender, the rocky, hilly landscape of southern Lebanon provides several advantages. The terrain, while allowing unrestricted dismounted movement, largely restricts armoured manoeuvre, channelling vehicles toward roads or other easily identifiable avenues of approach.

The importance of terrain, even in this period of modern warfare, was again demonstrated in the fighting in the south. Israel would fight Hezbollah on intricate physical terrain that Hezbollah understood and had organised in a sophisticated way for defence.

THE PATH TO WAR

The Blue Line

By June 2000, a UN cartographic team working with the United Nations Interim Force in Lebanon (UNIFIL) had established a new border line between Lebanon and Israel. Christened the "Blue Line," the 79-kilometre demarcation was fully endorsed by the UN Security Council on 18 June 2000. UNIFIL's highest priority was helping the Lebanese Government and its armed forces to assume their responsibilities along the border and throughout the area from which Israel had withdrawn. While certainly admirable in its intentions, the UN peace plan was doomed from the start.

Due to political constraints, the Lebanese central government could not commit its army to police the border in southern Lebanon. Further complicating the peace process was the fact that the Israeli withdrawal from Lebanon, in May 2000, was not total. Israeli army garrisons remained in parts of Lebanon, including Sha'ba Farms, Kafar Shuba Hills, and parts of Ghajar village. To Hezbollah, any Israeli presence in Lebanon was unacceptable. The Lebanese thought the land was theirs and were outraged over Israel's continued possession of this piece of territory.

The Situation

From 2000 to 2006, Hezbollah conducted many attacks into Israeli territory. Generally, the Israelis showed restraint in response to the provocations, while it dealt with what it believed were more pressing threats, like instability and violence in the disputed territories or growing Iranian influence in the Middle East. The United States, in the wake of the 2005 Cedar Revolution, also pressed for restraint towards Hezbollah, as it sought to nurture the growth of Lebanese autonomy and democracy following Syria's withdrawal. However, Israeli patience with Hezbollah had its limits.

Israeli leaders were growingly concerned over the build-up of Hezbollah rockets on its borders and the frequency of cross-border raids into Israel by both Hezbollah and Palestinian militants. Hezbollah's rising political power in Lebanon also worried the Israelis, for if their power continued to increase, they could eventually secure control over the Lebanese Armed Forces (LAF), giving the organisation a near-monopoly on military power within Lebanon and access to improved weaponry.

The Olmert government in Israel sought to improve Israeli national security by eliminating or significantly reducing the military and political power of Hezbollah. Israel intended to achieve these strategic ends by accomplishing three supporting goals:

(a) Destroy or seriously degrade Hezbollah's military strength, with a focus on its rocket arsenal.

(b) Reduce popular support for the organisation in Lebanon by convincing Lebanese Shias and other groups to turn on Hezbollah.

(c) Put pressure the Lebanese government to disarm Hezbollah and deploy the Lebanese Armed Forces to southern Lebanon to secure the borders.

Strategic Overview

Lieutenant General Dan Halutz, the Chief of the Israel Defence Forces' (IDF) General Staff and a former Israeli Air Force (IAF) pilot, had two plans for a war against Hezbollah. The first was Operation ***Stone of Fire*** which the Israelis had developed and refined since 2000. It called for several Army divisions to invade southern Lebanon and push Hezbollah 40 kilometres north to the Litani River, reducing the organisation's ability to strike Israel with rockets. The plan had significant drawbacks:

(a) A large Israeli occupation of southern Lebanon risked provoking regional and international condemnation for the inevitable destruction to civilian life and property that it would cause.

(b) A ground war risked more IDF casualties that would likely lead to increased domestic political pressure, just as it did during the occupation of southern Lebanon during the late 1990s.

(c) The plan had lost its relevance after Syria's military withdrew from Lebanon in 2005.

The second plan under consideration was a 48 to 72-hour bombing campaign, codenamed Operation *Ice Breaker*. It envisioned an aerial blitz that would attempt to destroy Hezbollah's entire military apparatus. General Halutz also believed that the size and scope of the campaign could convince the Lebanese people to turn on Hezbollah and disarm it. The IDF General Staff was so confident of an expanded version Operation *Ice Breaker* that they promised US officials a decisive Israeli victory within 35 days.

Israel's military strategy and planning rested on three assumptions:

(a) ***A large military operation could both destroy Hezbollah's military wing and erode popular support for the organisation.*** Military force, although appropriate for degrading Hezbollah's military power—at least in the short-term—risked undermining the second goal by increasing popular support for the organisation. Hezbollah's popularity originated from its history of fighting Israel and providing reconstruction aid and social services to its communities. Bombarding Hezbollah targets deeply embedded in civilian neighbourhoods worked in favour of Hezbollah's political strategy, by providing it the opportunity to play the role of Lebanon's defender against Israel, while also enabling it to act as first responders to the communities harmed by the fighting.

(b) ***Israel could quickly defeat Hezbollah with limited costs and commitments.*** The Israeli military had the means to destroy or seriously degrade Hezbollah's military capabilities, when given the necessary time and political support to do so; and three times in the past, Israel's small disciplined military, had withstood the combined power of nearly the entire Arab world. If Israel could successfully wage a multi-front war against multiple well-equipped armies, logically, the same force could handily defeat a group of militants. However, Hezbollah, in 2006, was a different kind of enemy; not a conventional army, like Israel's former Egyptian or Syrian adversaries, nor mostly unconventional, like Hamas. Hezbollah, a highly evolved militant organisation possessed a deadly combination of conventional and unconventional military capabilities. It also has a robust political wing that operates independently and within the Lebanese government. Israel did not anticipate the strengths and capabilities of this "hybrid" threat; consequently, it went to war overly-confident that it could vanquish

its enemy, who, as it discovered, was far more tenacious and capable than anticipated.

(c) ***Israel's military was ready for war with Hezbollah.*** On the eve of the conflict, Israeli Army personnel had little to no training or experience to fight an enemy as disciplined and capable as Hezbollah. After the 2000 withdrawal from Lebanon, the IDF focused on combating undisciplined, low-tech Palestinian militant groups. These militants, unlike Hezbollah, generally operated in small, lightly armed squads (about a dozen men) and lacked formal military training. A typical Israeli Army unit could easily outgun and outmanoeuvre most Palestinian militants. Hezbollah, on the other hand, had well-equipped fighters, trained in modern infantry and guerrilla tactics. By focusing their attention on Palestinian militants, Israeli soldiers became increasingly unprepared for combat against larger, more disciplined enemies.

The combat effectiveness of Israeli brigade and division level units also suffered from the post-2000 shift in priorities. Beginning in 2000, the IDF focused its training on small skirmishes and policing missions, not large combined-arms battles. Thus, few brigade and division commanders had significant training or experience commanding large units in training environments or in the real operations. Tank crews, for instance, had little or no experience operating their vehicles in open land combat. Many of them had spent more time as riflemen on foot patrols than they did inside their vehicles; and when they did fight from their vehicles, they operated more like pillboxes or armoured bulldozers. Israeli tank crews were, therefore, unprepared for combat with tanks while operating in open terrain that required large, complex manoeuvres. The focus on low intensity conflicts, which was necessary for confronting Hamas and similar groups, reduced the IDF from the formidable conventional fighting force that it was in the 20th century to an organisation that was best suited for stability operations. The IDF, essentially, had lost its ability to conduct effective full-spectrum operations.

In terms of equipment also, Israel was unprepared for war against Hezbollah. The Israelis had two distinct advantages over the militants: armour and airpower. Hezbollah understood that withstanding an Israeli assault meant countering these two advantages. In the inter-war years, Hezbollah addressed its disadvantage by purchasing advanced anti-tank guided missiles (ATGMs). It thus gained the ability to destroy any Israeli armoured vehicle, including the *Merkava* main battle tank (MBT)—the heaviest tank in the Israeli arsenal and, arguably, the best in the world. To counteract ATGMs, tanks require reactive armour plating, i.e. armoured plates that cover the outside of a tank. These plates explode off a tank as the heat of the incoming missile approaches, destroying or deflecting the threat before impact. Reactive armour plating is especially effective against ATGM fire. Unfortunately, the Israeli government decided against purchasing newer reactive armour plating. Thus, Israeli tanks and vehicles were extremely vulnerable to Hezbollah's newly-acquired ATGMs.

To address the challenge of Israeli airpower, Hezbollah engineers constructed intricate, heavily-fortified bunkers throughout the rolling hills and rocky ridges of southern Lebanon. From inside bunkers, Hezbollah militants could evade the IAF, store weapons, and move along covered and concealed routes to ambush Israeli ground units. Although strong, their fortifications could be destroyed. US bunker-busting bombs, which had proven effective in Iraq and Afghanistan, were available for the Israelis to purchase. These weapons, however, had little utility against Palestinian militants—the main focus of Israeli military operations prior to 2006. Because of this focus on low intensity conflicts, Israel did not stockpile these bombs. Hezbollah's construction of fortifications and deployment of ATGMs achieved their desired effects: Israeli armour lost its near invulnerability to Hezbollah arms and the influence of Israeli air superiority was diminished.

Hezbollah was, unlike Israel, highly prepared for war in southern Lebanon. Its fighters, who lived and operated among the towns that lined the Israeli border, almost craved war. With its fighters willing and enthusiastic for combat, Hezbollah had a defensive strategy that adhered to a simple formula for victory: force a heavy-handed Israeli response, exploit the outcome, and make the conflict untenable for Israeli soldiers and civilians through a relentless rocket assault on northern Israeli settlements. It meant surviving Israel's initial aerial onslaught, while maintaining a steady stream of rockets into Israel. By maintaining the rocket campaign and surviving the aerial assault, Hezbollah calculated that it could force Israel to mount a ground offensive to stop the rockets and destroy Hezbollah positions. Once in southern Lebanon, the IDF was entering Hezbollah territory, where the militants could inflict tremendous damage on their enemy from prepared defences, reducing the morale of the Israeli military, as it did in the 1990s. Forcing an Israeli ground incursion had the added benefit of reintroducing Israeli soldiers to southern Lebanon, which could rally public support behind Hezbollah, similar to what it did in the 1990s.

Psychological operations were a central element of Hezbollah's defence against Israel, targeting three primary audiences: the Israeli people, the Lebanese people, and the international community. To influence the Israeli people, Hezbollah relied on its rocket campaign. Hezbollah planners anticipated that they could reduce Israeli support for the war by making any Israeli victory a pyrrhic one. To manipulate Lebanese public opinion, which the Israelis were trying to influence through firepower, Hezbollah relied on its extensive social services networks and media outlets. Its social services networks would care for civilian victims of the war and its media network would spread propaganda over the airwaves. To influence the international community, Hezbollah would broadcast images of death and destruction caused by the Israeli military strikes. These images could engender sympathy for Hezbollah and outrage against Israel, especially in the Muslim world, where Israel was already extremely unpopular.

Hezbollah's Preparations for the War

Since the 1990s, Hezbollah cultivated strong support in Lebanon, especially in the southern Shia areas. This support has enabled it to build a strong political and military organisation. Politically, Hezbollah used their support in southern Lebanon to increase its power and influence at the national level. Militarily, the organisation gained a sympathetic population to operate amongst during confrontations with Israel. With strong popular support, militants defending the towns and villages of southern Lebanon blended in among civilians and attacked when and where they chose.

South of the Litani River, Hezbollah's 2,000 to 3,000 fighters fell under three sector commands. Within these commands, Hezbollah commanders oversaw the construction of an intricate and concealed bunker system that gave Hezbollah defence in-depth, integrating its command centres, weapons depots, and rocket systems into towns and homes of its supporters. When it was time to launch, the operators knocked down a false wall, firing the rocket from inside the house. This tactic had the added benefit of limiting the IDF from striking most launch sites, given the difficulty in detecting the systems that remained concealed from aerial observation under the roofs of the houses. At the same time, striking these rockets within civilian houses, risked producing collateral damage that Hezbollah could then exploit in their psychological operations campaign.

Operating in this manner ensured Hezbollah's enemies came under persistent fire and observation while in southern Lebanon. It also avoided concentrating forces that Israel could strike with its superior firepower. These bunkers also utilised the terrain to their advantage. Hezbollah engineers positioned many of their bunkers along ridgelines that overlook the exposed routes that the Israelis had to traverse to invade southern Lebanon. These tactically important positions allowed the entrenched militants to track Israeli ground and air movements, anticipate their intentions, and set up improvised explosive devices (IEDs) and ambushes along their routes. From dominating positions, forward observers could track approaching Israeli columns and call in accurate mortar fire. Coordinating the defence was a network of advanced aboveground and underground command and control centres that Hezbollah's Iranian allies helped build, staff, and maintain. Due to Hezbollah's superior knowledge of the terrain and highly prepared defensive positions, the Israeli invasion force in southern Lebanon faced a daunting gauntlet of coordinated ambushes, artillery attacks, and IEDs.

Also working in Hezbollah's favour was the fact that the stakes in the war were much higher for them than for Israel. Defeat for Hezbollah could have resulted in the total destruction of their military wing, reduced their influence in the Lebanese government, and the reoccupation of their land by Israeli troops. For Israel, on the other hand, defeat essentially meant the return to the status quo of the previous six years. Thus, Hezbollah could muster a stronger will to combat than Israel. It meant Israel's vision of dismantling the organisation quickly was highly unrealistic, for they lacked the necessary political willpower to achieve these objectives, which would that require far more time and blood than Israel was willing to expend.

Hezbollah's operational design was based on the presumption that Israel no longer had a tolerance for war and its inevitable butcher's bill. Building on this premise, Hezbollah was convinced that, in any future war, Israel would rely heavily on air and artillery precision weapons and limit its use of ground forces.

The defensive network built by Hezbollah in southern Lebanon was an engineering marvel. Hezbollah's robust and hardened defences were the result of six years of diligent work, after the Israeli withdrawal from the region in 2000. Many of the command bunkers designed and built by Hezbollah engineers were fortified, and a few were even air-conditioned. The digging of the arsenals had been accompanied by a programme of deception, with some bunkers being constructed in the open and often under the eyes of Israeli drone vehicles or under the observation of Lebanese citizens with close ties to the Israelis. With few exceptions, these bunkers were decoys. The building of other bunkers went forward in areas kept hidden from the Lebanese population. The most important command bunkers and weapons-arsenal bunkers were dug deeply into Lebanon's rocky hills—to a depth of 40 metres. Nearly 600 separate ammunition and weapons bunkers were strategically prepared in the region south of the Litani. For security reasons, no single commander knew the location of each bunker and each distinct Hezbollah militia unit was assigned access to three bunkers only—a primary munitions bunker and two reserve bunkers, in case the primary bunker was destroyed. Separate primary and backup marshalling points were also designated for the distinct combat units, which were tasked to arm and fight within specific combat areas. The security protocols for the marshalling of troops was diligently maintained. Although the Israeli intelligence community believed Hezbollah's defensive network was based on Iranian military doctrine, other sources suggests the elaborate system was based on "a defensive guerrilla force organised along North Korean lines. Evidence suggests that the Iranian Revolutionary Guard was also heavily involved in the construction effort.

Between 2000 and 2006, Hezbollah also mastered the art of counter-signals intelligence (C-SIGNET), a capability that could pay huge dividends. In the human intelligence (HUMINT) arena, Hezbollah also proved highly successful. Working with Lebanese intelligence officers, Hezbollah managed to turn Israeli agents in southern Lebanon and dismantle a sizable Israeli spy ring. In a few crucially important cases, Hezbollah senior intelligence officials were able to feedback false information on their militia's most important emplacements to Israel with the result that Israel target folders identified key emplacements that did not, in fact, exist. It also appears likely that Hezbollah succeeded in placing its own agents in northern Israel.

The key to defeating Israel required Hezbollah to modify its doctrine. By the early summer of 2006, Hezbollah had transformed its original 13

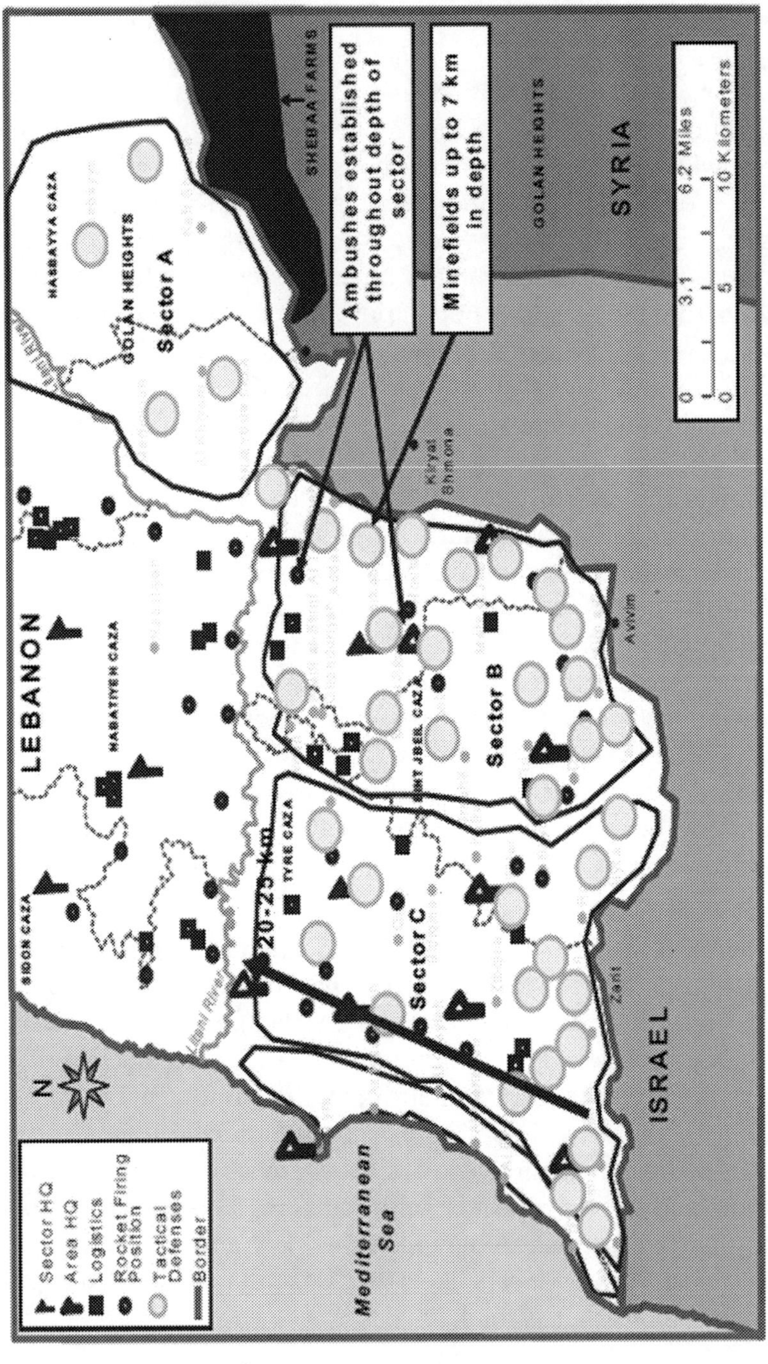

Map 3: Hezbollah Defensive System in Southern Lebanon

principles of warfare (a doctrine that had worked brilliantly during the course of the Israeli occupation of Lebanon) into a new and unique design. Hezbollah's new model combined both guerrilla and conventional methods, in many ways mirroring the approach adopted by the North Vietnamese and Viet Cong during their long war with the US. Hezbollah was able to efficiently adjust its tactics and operational design. Its planning was simple and inspired.

Hezbollah designed a war in which presumably Israel could only choose which soft underbelly to expose: the one whereby it avoids a ground operation and exposes its home front vulnerability, or the one whereby it enters Lebanon and sustains the loss of soldiers in ongoing ground-based attrition with a guerrilla organisation. Hezbollah apparently left Israel with two undesirable options. At the tactical level, Hezbollah addressed the IDF's precision weapons capability by reducing its own weapon signature and target-appearance time and then building hardened defensive positions. Knowing full well that the IDF desired to generate effects on its systems, Hezbollah created a network of autonomous cells with little inter-cell systemic interaction. On the strategic level, Hezbollah also predicted that the IDF would attack with long-range precision weapons on its strategic centres of gravity. To counter this, Hezbollah simply did away with them. In any future war with Israel, there would be no critical strategic asset to attack.

Israeli Preparations for the War

Within months of the IDF's withdrawal from Lebanon in 2000, Israel faced a Palestinian uprising in the West Bank and Gaza Strip. Known as the Second Intifada, the insurrection produced a massive strain on the Israeli military, particularly the ground forces. As a result, fewer recruits received suitable training, resulting in a combat force ill-prepared for the challenges ahead. The Palestinian revolt also had a deleterious effect on officers who had little experience with military operations, other than counterinsurgency warfare.

While Israel continued to deal with a fairly constant stream of Hezbollah provocation on its northern border, unlike its massive response to the Palestinian uprising, it remained reluctant to conduct any extensive retaliation against Hezbollah. Many individuals in Israel contend that Prime Minister Ehud Barak did not want to intensify actions against

Hezbollah, as this would equate to acknowledging he was wrong in withdrawing from southern Lebanon in the first place. Prime Minister Ariel Sharon, who replaced Barak, had been driven out of politics for his role in the 1982 invasion of Lebanon. After nearly 20 years in the political wilderness, he had no intention of involving Israel in another war there.

During this time, the Israelis also formulated a new doctrine. In the years following its withdrawal from southern Lebanon, the IDF began to embrace the theories of precision firepower, Effects-Based Operations (EBO), and Systemic Operational Design (SOD). EBO emerged out of the Network-Centric Warfare (NCW) concept in 2001, with the publication of a white paper by the US Joint Forces Command (JFCOM). At its core, EBO is designed to affect the cognitive domain of the enemy and his systems, rather than annihilating his forces.

EBO are part of an amorphous body of thought that emerged from US Air Force doctrinal work, think tank studies, and the JFCOM in the 1990s. It has its roots in belief that the advent of the information age and of precision-guided munitions would allow a military force to destroy specific portions of its enemy with incredible precision. Further, EBO theory held that the target of these attacks ought not to be traditional front-line ground or air forces but, instead, should be key command and control, logistics, radars, transportation, and related capabilities whose destruction will render the enemy incapable of employing his military forces and unable to accomplish his military objectives. An important secondary benefit often-cited was the reduction in military casualties and collateral damage by the accuracy of new weapons and the avoidance of extensive ground battles.

Proponents of EBO and other theorists buttressed their claims by citing the dominant role of air power in the Iraq War of 1990–91 and in the Bosnian and Kosovo campaigns of the late-1990s. Although they differed in the particulars, EBO proponents generally agreed that it would be possible for nations to use precision firepower, delivered primarily from the air, to destroy discrete targets within an enemy's leadership and C^2 systems, and that doing so would then make it possible to achieve one's strategic objectives without the need to resort to traditional ground operations focused on the destruction of the enemy's main forces or the need to capture and hold territory. EBO proponents within the IDF came to believe that an enemy could be completely immobilised by precision air attacks against critical military systems. The Israeli supporters of EBO also hypothesised that little or no land forces would be required since it would not be necessary to destroy the enemy.

Brigadier General Shimon Naveh's SOD was a tool intended to help IDF commanders plan their campaigns. Naveh founded the IDF's Operational Theory Research Institute (OTRI) in 1995. After years of work within the OTRI, SOD attempted to provide commanders with the aptitude necessary to think critically, systemically and methodologically about war fighting. The design focused on the concept of the 'enemy' and provide operational commanders with tools to conceptualise both their enemies and themselves for the purpose of designing suitable campaigns.

For the IDF, the major problem with SOD was the new terminology and methodology. Many IDF officers could not understand why the old system of simple orders and terminology was being replaced by a design that few could understand. After several alterations and revisions, the new IDF doctrine was endorsed and signed by the Chief of the IDF General Staff, Lieutenant General Dan Halutz, in April 2006. Halutz was the first IAF officer ever appointed Chief of the IDF General Staff. On the first page of the document, Halutz wrote, "*Familiarity with and use of the concept of operation are the key to our success in warfare, in which the only option available is victory. Therefore, the commanding officers of the IDF must understand, assimilate and implement what is written there when they call their forces into action and prepare them for their goal*". It is possible that not even Halutz understood the document he endorsed and signed. The new doctrine was designed to cover strategy, force transformation, EBO as well as introducing a new military lexicon and new structure for staff work methodology, battlefield analysis and orders structure and contents. The borders between EBO and SOD were blurred in this doctrine.

The new doctrine replaced the old structure of Mission, Commander's Intent, Forces and Tasks with a whole new phraseology of Political Directive, Strategic Purpose, System Boundaries, Operational Boundaries, Campaign's Organising Theme, Opposing System Rationale etc. Field commanders did not like the new doctrine, principally because they did not understand it. Many experienced officers could not comprehend most of 170-pages long document. The terminology used was felt to be too complicated to be understood by the officers who had to implement it. The doctrine was supposed to be limited to the higher levels of command, while at the theatre/division level, the old terminology and methodology should have been used. Nonetheless, it trickled down. Commanders need to speak in a simple accessible manner, composed essentially of two things: what do we defend and what do we attack. When an order is given to render the enemy "incoherent" or to make the enemy feel "distress" or "chased down," or to "achieve standoff domination of the theatre" field commanders simply cannot gauge progress. Nevertheless, very few IDF officers stepped forward to voice their concerns.

Above all, the IDF was stretched by budgetary cuts to the ground forces and the continuing demands placed on them by the Palestinian uprising. To make matters worse, soldiers with perishable combat skills, such as tank crews, patrolled the West Bank and Gaza Strip, in the *intifada*. Reservist tank crews received little training. A tank reservist was required to complete a five-day refresher exercise each year. Most hardly got that in the course of three years, others in the space of five, and yet others none at all. The IDF also made sizable cuts in the reserve ground forces' budget and equipment. The quality of the equipment sent a message about values to the reserve soldiers. Even more disturbing than the reserves cuts and the breakdown of skills at the tactical level was the fact that many high-ranking IDF officers, both regular and reserve, had not received adequate training. Brigade commanders were under-trained, and commanders above brigade level did not command their units in training for years. This was not the result of neglect or omission, but of intentional policy.

Under the IDF's new doctrine, the corps formation was eliminated, and plans were in the works to also abolish the division when the war erupted in 2006. The SOD did not see a role for land formations larger than a brigade. Instead of killing the enemy, they wanted to create a 'consciousness of victory' on own side and 'cognitive perception of defeat' on the other side.

Against this backdrop, Halutz remained supremely confident that the IDF could defeat any enemy who had the audacity to attack Israel.

The Spark

On 27 June 2006, the IDF issued a high alert along a portion of the border known as milepost 105 near the village of Zarit, Israel. At this location, the road dipped down into a low *wadi* or valley, making it impossible for nearby observation posts and dug-in tanks to see IDF-mounted patrols as they made their rounds. Certain that Hezbollah had something in the offing,

Israeli intelligence placed an elite *Egoz* reconnaissance unit in ambush positions at milepost 105. By 2 July, however, no incursion materialised and the *Egoz* team withdrew from the area. On that same day, the alert level was lowered to "heightened" and, on 10 July, was reduced to just above "normal." The IDF reserve soldiers in the vicinity of milepost 105 returned to routine patrol duties and looked forward to the end of their reserve obligation. This reserve battalion was part of Brigade 300, Division 91, commanded by Brigadier General Gal Hirsch. Interestingly, the division commander had warned the IDF General Staff that the reserve battalion was not fit to operate along the northern border and demanded they be replaced with trained soldiers. The General Staff rejected his request.

On the night of 11 July, IDF monitors picked up several reports of contact along the electronic border fence near milepost 105. An IDF reserve patrol also reported around 20 Hezbollah fighters near the same location. Amazingly, it appears this information never filtered down to the reserve soldiers preparing to conduct the day patrol in the area.

On 12 July 2006, Hezbollah commandos moved across the border to milepost 105 between the villages of Zar'it and Shetula in northern Israel. This position offered Hezbollah an ideal location for mounting an ambush. To reduce the likelihood of detection further, Hezbollah snipers in south Lebanon engaged and destroyed surveillance cameras along the border roads. Small groups of fighters also launched a series of diversionary attacks that distracted Israeli quick reaction forces that were mustering along the border.

East of the kill zone, a pair of Israeli *Humvees* carrying eight reservists, just hours from ending their tour of duty, headed toward the ambush site. As the *Humvees* closed on the ambush site, the lead vehicle struck a large IED, initiating the ambush. Rocket propelled grenades (RPGs) ripped through the thin armour of the lead *Humvee*, engulfing the crewmembers in an inferno. Amid the smoke and confusion, several ambushers rushed and snatched Staff Sergeants Goldwasser and Regev, who had been wounded, and withdrew across the border before Israeli reinforcements arrived. Hezbollah's Operation ***Truthful Promise*** had succeeded.

The situation was so chaotic that the IDF battalion commander responsible for the area did not realise until 0927 hours that Hezbollah had abducted two of his soldiers. Once the situation became clear, he promptly broadcast the code word *Hannibal* to all IDF forces in the

Northern Command, indicating an Israeli soldier had been kidnapped. Ideally, the issuing of this code word would have set in motion a chain of pre-planned events designed to rescue kidnapped IDF soldiers.

Upon issuing the code word, the battalion commander was to move his forces rapidly into Lebanon and attempt to cut off Hezbollah's escape routes. This movement never materialised. Concerned with mines and IEDs, he chose not to advance. By 0933 hours, however, certain portions of *Hannibal* were put into motion. Artillery fire onto Hezbollah positions went ahead as planned but was executed only partially and with long delays. By 0939 hours, IDF attack helicopters arrived at milepost 105 where they found the smouldering wreckage of the *Humvees* but no sign of Hezbollah fighters.

It was not until 1003 hours that the battalion commander reported the specifics of the kidnapping to his brigade headquarters, i.e. 57 minutes later, and at 1100 hours, a few armoured vehicles crossed into Lebanon. As they moved toward a hill overlooking a possible Hezbollah escape route, a massive IED exploded beneath a *Merkava* 4 tank, instantly killing the crew of four. As rescue teams rushed forward to retrieve the bodies of the dead tank crew, two other IDF soldiers died during a vicious firefight with Hezbollah. At 1200 hours, the IDF high command issued an order called the *Fourth Dimension*, activating air strikes on 69 bridges in southern Lebanon. These strikes were meant to impede the kidnappers' escape.

The IDF's response to the Hezbollah incursion and kidnapping was a muddled, haphazard affair. From the failure to disseminate intelligence, to the lackadaisical approach of the soldiers on patrol, and the failure to rapidly pursue Hezbollah fighters, the operation revealed a stunning ineptitude on the part of the soldiers and leadership within the IDF.

Around mid-afternoon on 12 July, Chief of the IDF General Staff Dan Halutz, Israeli Prime Minister Yossi Olmert, and Defence Minister Amir Peretz seized control of the situation and began planning their response to the kidnapping. Both Olmert and Peretz had limited backgrounds in military affairs. Olmert had served as an IDF newspaper reporter, while Peretz fulfilled his military obligation as a maintenance officer. The Defence Minister did not have knowledge or experience in military, political or governmental matters. He also did not have knowledge of the basic principles of using military force to achieve political goals. In formulating their response to the kidnapping, both Olmert and Peretz were forced to

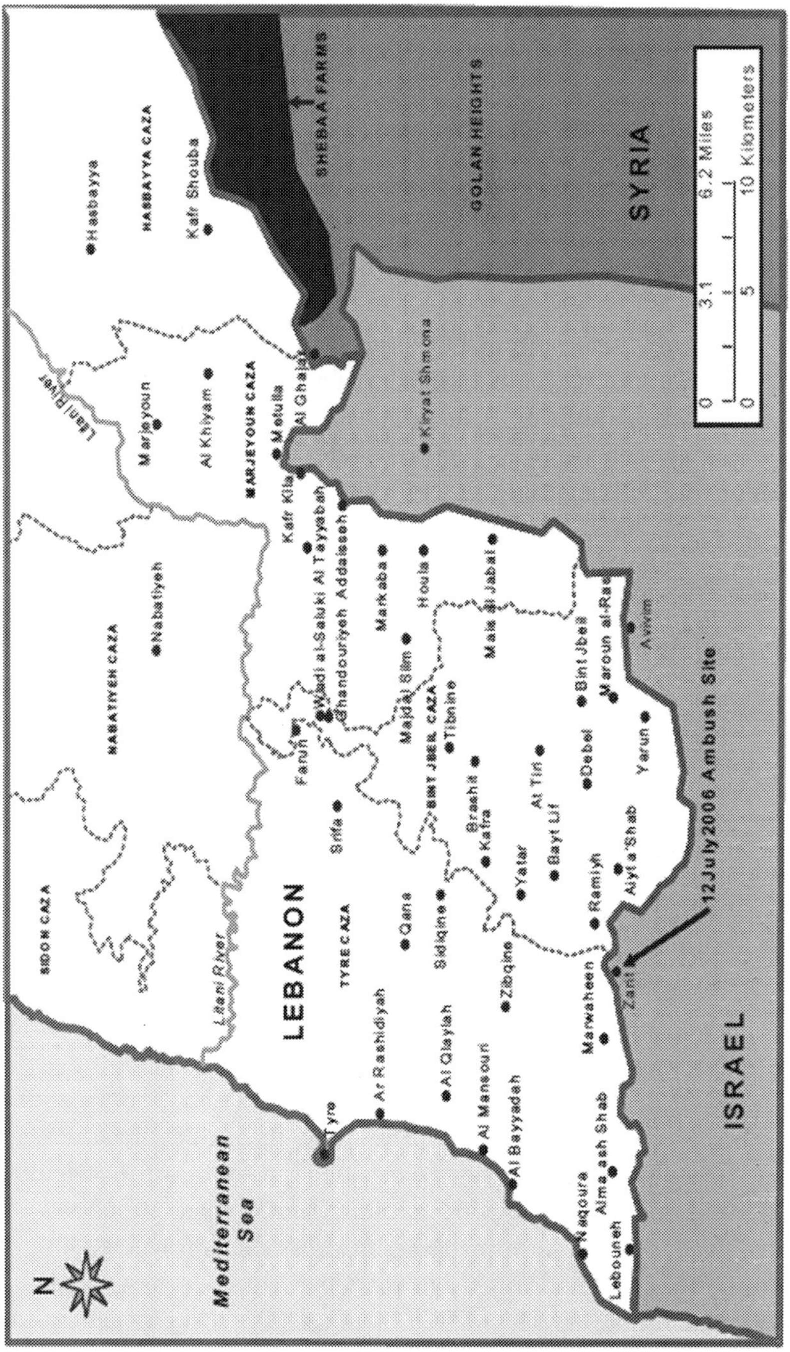

Map 4: The Ambush Site

rely heavily on Halutz, a general who in every respect was unprepared for a full-scale ground war with Hezbollah.

The motives behind the 12 July kidnapping remain unclear. It was certainly not designed to provoke a war with Israel. A form of pressure to force the release of captured militants and sympathisers imprisoned in Israeli jails could be a more plausible explanation. Nasrallah perhaps assessed that the conflict would not expand beyond the raid and limited Israeli reprisals.

Israeli Prime Minister Ehud Olmert faced intense public pressure to retaliate after the raid, which occurred only a month after the kidnapping of Corporal Gailad Shalit by Palestinian militants along the Gaza Strip. In a televised speech delivered shortly after the raid, Olmert rejected Hezbollah's proposed negotiations. He proclaimed that Israel would punish Hezbollah for its "act of war" with "a very painful and far-reaching response."

Halutz convinced Olmert and Peretz that Israel should strike back against Hezbollah and the Lebanese central government with a substantial air campaign. The plan was not designed to directly or fully crush Hezbollah's capabilities but to produce "effects" that would force Hezbollah out of southern Lebanon and cause them to disarm. Halutz proposed an immense air strike against "symbolic" Lebanese targets and Hezbollah's military resources. The plan also called for targeted strikes against Hezbollah's military and political leadership. Hezbollah, however, had prepared for an effects-based campaign, and the Lebanese government was too weak and incapable of challenging Hezbollah. There was simply no lever to pull that would cause Hezbollah to crumple.

The stage was now set to reveal to the world Israeli high-tech fantasies and basic unpreparedness. On the night of 12 July, Israeli jets and artillery began limited attacks on infrastructure targets across Lebanon, Hezbollah's rockets, command and control centres, and its mouthpiece, *al-Manar* television. Just after midnight, an IAF squadron flying in the vicinity of Beirut attacked and destroyed 54 Hezbollah *Zelzal* rocket launchers. When Halutz received word of the mission's success, he informed Olmert by secure phone that all the long-range rockets have been destroyed. Israel would soon learn that his declaration of mission accomplished could not have been further from the truth.

Hezbollah Strikes Back

Nasrallah was completely taken aback by the massive Israeli bombardment. In fact, during an interview after the war, he admitted that Hezbollah had made a terrible mistake in capturing two IDF soldiers and killing eight others on the morning of 12 July 2006. On 14 July though, after the IAF attacks on the Beirut airport and after the Israeli Navy blockaded all of Lebanon, Nasrallah delivered a taped message to the press. He invited listeners to look to the sea, and with perfect theatrical timing an explosion on the horizon rocked the INS Hanit, an Israeli naval vessel that was hit by an Iranian-produced C-802 *Noor* guided missile. The missile blasted a hole in the ship and killed four of its crew. The *Eilat* (Sa'ar 5)-class missile corvette had failed to activate its defence system against radar-guided anti-ship missiles. The Israelis were not aware that Hezbollah possessed this kind of missile. This was an early hint that Hezbollah might have been better prepared than Israel presumed.

Outraged over the bold attack, Israeli Prime Minister Ehud Olmert authorised a large-scale military retaliation against Hezbollah. The unprovoked raid provided Olmert with an opportunity to deal a major blow to a long-time Israeli adversary. Through military action, the Olmert government sought to destroy Hezbollah's military capabilities and convince the Lebanese government and people to disarm the organisation and abandon their support for it. Israeli military planners initially believed that they could quickly achieve Olmert's stated objectives through an air and sea campaign, backed by limited ground forces.

OPPOSING FORCES

Israeli Perceptions of the Security Environment

The absence of a high-end threat to Israel, combined with the demands on the IDF to deal with the Second *Intifada* (and with the IDF's forced removal of Israeli settlers from Gaza in 2005), significantly affected the strategic and operational perspectives of Israeli politicians and military. Some reached the conclusion that Israel is beyond the era of wars and that it had enough military might and superiority to deter others from declaring war against her and the main challenge facing the land forces would be low-intensity asymmetrical conflicts. The result was a LIC-centric mindset.

The Israeli Army was the service most affected by this view of the security situation, particularly because LIC requirements had stretched it significantly and budget cuts had been implemented. Furthermore, because the Israeli Army believed its future demands were going to involve LIC, it understandably focused on preparing for this type of conflict. Consequently, high-end combat training was not deemed important. The operational environment and reduced training funds combined to produce a view that fighting the *intifada* was all the training needed by ground units. Also, because active-duty Israeli Army units were principally responsible for ongoing LIC operations, which were mainly carried out by brigades, reserve training and higher-level (e.g., division-level and above) exercises were curtailed. Armoured-unit training was neglected as those units were deemed largely irrelevant in LIC. Finally, the Israeli Army assigned its best officers to deal with LIC threats in the West Bank and Gaza, further reinforcing the focus on LIC.

Like the Israeli Army, the IAF was also heavily engaged in fighting the Second *Intifada* and in confronting the challenges of LIC. It was considered the principal means of deterring and hedging against the unlikely possibility of a state-on-state war and of carrying out possible strikes against Iranian nuclear capabilities. Thus, it had to maintain a mix of low- and high-end capabilities. For LIC, the IAF had made significant adaptations in its munitions, command and control, and intelligence systems, and adopted new methods of air operations. The goal was to be able to hit the target (and only the target), minimising collateral damage and the killing of innocent civilians.

In the IDF, almost all aviation assets are owned by the IAF, including UAVs, attack and utility helicopters (including those used for medical evacuation), and fixed-wing aircraft. By 2006, the IAF had become quite adept at supporting the Israeli Army in LIC contexts, particularly in using attack helicopters to pinpoint and eliminate hostile forces. The IAF's capacity to support large-scale air-ground operations—particularly in the area of close air support (mostly fixed-wing close air support)—was neglected. Air-control teams were removed from Israeli Army brigades and there was little, if any, joint training, given the absence of a threat that would require that the IDF be ready to employ this kind of capability.

IDF Deficiencies on the Eve of the Second Lebanon War

In 2006, the IDF had a number of key deficiencies:

- It was in the early stages of incorporating a new operational concept that was highly reliant on Systemic Operational Design (SOD) and standoff fires (provided by both air and artillery) to change the opponent's will. There was no clear understanding of whether this approach would have success against an adversary like Hezbollah. Importantly, understanding of the IDF's operational concept was not yet fully institutionalised.
- Intelligence about Hezbollah was highly compartmentalised and not generally available to operational commanders and planners. Also, the level of intelligence that the IDF had become accustomed to having in the West Bank and Gaza was not available in Lebanon.
- The Israeli Army was largely unprepared to carry out high-intensity, combined-arms fire and-manoeuvre operations.
- The IAF and the Israeli Army had not trained or organised for joint air-ground operations.
- Neither the IAF nor the Israeli Army had a clear understanding of how to address the persistent short-range rocket attacks that Hezbollah

launched against Israel once the war commenced. Additionally, Northern Command, the responsible headquarters during the war, had no operational plans for dealing with these attacks once they began.

- Israeli political and military leaders did not, apparently, understand Hezbollah's strategy of "not losing is winning."

Israeli Orbat

The Northern Territorial Command at Safed had overall responsibility for ground operations in Lebanon. Control of ground operations in the immediate border area was the responsibility of the Galilee Division. As additional reserve forces were mobilised and deployed to the border area, Northern Territorial Command exercised operational control over them. These long-standing arrangements had been employed in previous conflicts with Syria and in Lebanon.

IAF headquarters in Tel Aviv controlled air operations over Lebanon and also had overall responsibility for heliborne commando operations deep in Lebanon. The IAF, built for a major war with the Arab states, had more than enough capacity for its missions in Lebanon.

The Israeli navy was responsible for operations off the coast of Lebanon and for coastal operations by the Sea Commandos, Israel's naval special warfare unit. Israel's navy was heavily committed to the Lebanon conflict, conducting the largest and most sustained operation in its history. Activity by all components of the IDF were coordinated by IDF headquarters in Tel Aviv, where major decisions on the conduct of the war were made.

The IDF could call upon a very large range of assets for the war, even while conducting operations on the Gaza front. Even before mobilisation, Israel had available several regular infantry and armoured brigades in the north. It was able to induct additional regular units to the area, and once mobilisation of reserves began several additional divisions were available. These forces provided Israel with all the potential ground combat power needed for a large-scale operation. The numbers of Israeli forces involved grew steadily over the course of the conflict. Israel clearly enjoyed a substantial numerical advantage over Hezbollah in terms of available troops; however, the manner in which Israel committed its forces, especially early on, limited the significance of this advantage.

Israel had available some, perhaps most, of its best troops for the conflict. Elements of several elite reconnaissance and commando units were involved in the fighting. All of the IDF's high-quality parachute and infantry brigades were eventually committed, as were several high-quality regular armoured brigades. Much of the ground war would in fact be fought by those units, although reserve brigades performed major roles as the fighting wore on. In large measure the ground fighting would pit Israel's best against Hezbollah's best. Israeli ground Order of Battle is at Table 1. Asterisks in table data indicate uncertainty regarding unit designation.

Table 1: Israeli Ground Order of Battle

Unit	Type	Status	Operational area	Comment
Northern Territorial Command	Headquarters	Regular	Northern Israel, Lebanon, Golan Heights, Syrian front	Udi Adam—relieved of command during the conflict
Galilee Division	Headquarters	Regular	Lebanese border	Controlled early stage of ground operations
300 Brigade	Infantry	Regular	Western sector	Under Galilee Division
162 Armoured Division	Armour	Regular*	Western sector	Fought at Saluki Gorge
401 Armoured Brigade	Armour	Regular	Unknown	Under 162 Armoured Division
36 Armoured Division*	Armour	Regular	–	Golan Heights Division
7 Armoured Brigade	Armour	Regular	Eastern sector of Lebanon front	Under 36 Armoured Division
188 "Barak" Brigade*	Armour	Regular	Unknown	Under 36 Armoured Division
85 Armoured Division*	Armour	Reserve*	–	–
Golani Infantry Brigade	Infantry	Regular	Lebanese border	
13 Infantry Battalion	Infantry	Regular	–	Under Golani Infantry Brigade
51 Infantry Battalion	Infantry	Regular	Western sector	Under Golani Infantry Brigade
35 Paratroop Brigade*	Paratroop	Regular	Lebanese border	
101 Paratroop Batallion	Paratroop	Regular	Lebanese border	Under 35 Paratroop Brigade
226 Paratroop Battalion*	Paratroop	Regular	Lebanese border	Under 35 Paratroop Brigade
890 Paratroop Battalion	Paratroop	Regular	Lebanese border	Under 35 Paratroop Brigade
551 Paratroop Brigade*	Paratroop	Reserve	Lebanese border	
Nahal Brigade	Infantry	Regular	Western sector of Lebanon border	High-quality infantry unit; Battalion 931 identified

Unit	Type	Status	Operational area	Comment
931 Battalion				
"Givati" Infantry Brigade	Infantry	Regular	Western sector	Southern Territorial Command formation—in southern Lebanon
2 "Alexaroni" Brigade*	Infantry	Reserve	–	–
"Karmeli" Brigade	Infantry*	Reserve	–	–
"Herev" Battalion	Infantry	Regular	–	Druze*; under Galilee Division
Sayeret Matkal, General Headquarters (GHQ) Reconnaissance Unit	Reconnaissance and Raiding	Regular		Elite special operations unit under IDF GHQ
"Sayeret Egoz" (Walnut) Reconnaissance Unit	Reconnaissance and Raiding	Regular		Special operations unit under Golani Infantry Brigade
"Shayetet 13" Naval Commandos	Reconnaissance and Raiding	Regular	Primarily coastal operations	Israeli navy special warfare unit
"Sayeret Yael" (Ibex) special purpose engineering unit	Engineers	Regular*	As needed	Combat engineering unit; deep operations again infrastructure targets and fortified positions
Northern Command Artillery brigade*	Artillery	–	–	–
"Keren" Artillery Battalion	Artillery	Regular	–	Under Galilee Division
"Eyal" Artillery Battalion	Artillery	Reserve	–	–
Multiple Rocket Launcher System (MRLS) battalion*	Artillery	–	–	–
847 Brigade*	–	Reserve	–	–

The Israeli strategic concept focused on:

(a) Damaging Hezbollah's capabilities, primarily destroying its mid and long-range launch systems;

(b) Causing severe damage to components of Hezbollah's other military capabilities (i.e. other launch capabilities, targeted assassinations of senior personnel, command centres, previously identified logistical centres and warehouses, infrastructure and fortifications near the border, and civilian infrastructure serving the organisation's war systems);

(c) Damaging Hezbollah's image as "Lebanon's defender" and stressing its being the cause of massive damage to the country;

(d) Carrying out special operations in the rear of Hezbollah's strategic alignments;

(e) Intercepting and foiling arms shipments from Iran and Syria and through Syria to Hezbollah;

(f) Establishing a naval siege and no-fly zone to prevent aid from reaching Hezbollah; and

(g) Highlighting the responsibility of the Lebanese government for what was happening in the country.

The strategic objectives and concepts were formulated during the fighting. They were not accompanied by an analytical situation assessment on definition of the problem and objective, or judgment on the best way to use force to achieve that objective. Even after some far-reaching goals were defined, the high command and the government did not officially declare a shift to a state of war. On the contrary, the government imposed limits on the IDF's use of force; in particular, it banned direct, intentional damage to Lebanese state infrastructure (because of Prime Minister Olmert's commitment to President Bush, designed to allow the US a sphere of political action in order to reach a political settlement).

Hezbollah Readiness

Hezbollah had been preparing for a conflict with Israel ever since the Israeli withdrawal from southern Lebanon in May 2000. Hezbollah took advantage of the difficult terrain in southern Lebanon in developing its defences. From 2000 onwards, it began to build a network of bunkers, trenches, tunnels, and fighting positions across southern Lebanon, both in the villages and in the nature reserves. The bunkers were often quite sophisticated and well-equipped with electricity, phone lines, air conditioning, and stores for food, water, weapons, and ammunition. Most had a sleeping area, a kitchen, and a bathroom. The structures were built with Iranian, and possibly North Korean, help. Some bunkers were 20–30 metres underground and featured rocket-firing positions. They were constructed in great secrecy along the Israeli-Lebanese border, with their entrances camouflaged. The walls and ceilings were often reinforced with steel plates and girders painted black to prevent stray reflections from the sun from giving away the concealed entrance. The hilltop villages in southern Lebanon were often de facto fortresses that offered cover, concealment, and clear fields of fire to Hezbollah defenders.

Hezbollah's leaders came to the conclusion that the organisation would be best served by focusing fighter training on unconventional means, with an emphasis on operating individually and in small groups. Hezbollah trained its units in guerrilla warfare tactics (e.g., ambushes, attack and withdrawal).

In 2006, the Israelis estimated that Hezbollah had 10,000 fighters. Although it was active throughout Lebanon, Hezbollah was concentrated in southern Lebanon, Beirut, and Baalbek. Hezbollah's headquarters were located in the Dahiye neighbourhood of the Shia section of Beirut. The majority of Hezbollah's fighters were located in the Nabatieh region and south of the Litani River. The military command structure of Hezbollah is at Table 2.

Table 2: Hezbollah Military Command Structure

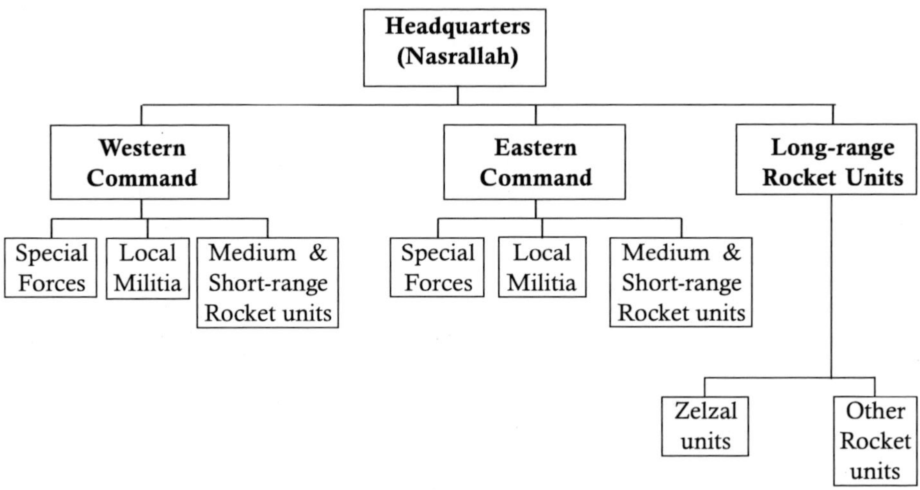

Hezbollah was organised in a cellular manner in southern Lebanon. The IR [Islamic Resistance, Hezbollah's military wing] was split into several sectors, each one consisting of between 12 and 15 villages. Each sector was sub-divided into smaller components of two to three villages. All sectors remained in close contact with each other, and the IR leadership in Beirut, using sophisticated fibre-optic communications that resisted IDF jamming and interception measures. Each sector had the power to act autonomously, if communications were severed, although IR's chain of command remained unbroken throughout the conflict. On the sub-sector level, fighters used Motorola walkie-talkies. Each fighter was issued a code number and communicated using an ad hoc code based on local and personal knowledge of each other that would be meaningless to an eavesdropper.

The IR forces on the ground in south Lebanon were split essentially into two wings. The first was the full-time military force of experienced, well-trained, highly disciplined and motivated guerrilla fighters, aged from their late twenties to late thirties. Numbering a few hundred, they were deployed in the network of bunkers and tunnels in south Lebanon as well as other locations. These fighters, equipped with military uniforms, were split into teams of 15 to 20 and were mainly responsible for artillery rockets, advanced anti-tank missiles and sniping.

The second wing was the "village guard" units, many of them veteran guerrilla combatants from the 1990s when the IDF occupied south Lebanon. Although they shared the same high degree of motivation and discipline as their full-time comrades, the village guards were an irregular force of part-time personnel. They had remained in their villages after most civilians had fled north. In the event of an IDF ground invasion, they were to provide successive layers of defence, taking advantage of their intimate knowledge of the local terrain to interdict and frustrate the IDF advance. Dressed in civilian clothing, they were armed with AK-47 assault rifles, light machine guns, rocket-propelled grenades and AT-3 *Sagger* anti-tank missiles.

Hezbollah fighters sometimes wore Israeli military uniforms to deceive and confuse the Israelis. Using Hezbollah's extensive network of trenches, tunnels, and bunkers for cover and for stockpiling weapons and supplies, Hezbollah fighters waited for Israeli patrols to approach. Once IDF soldiers advanced inside a village, Hezbollah personnel used surprise and close proximity to inflict damage on the Israelis. Often, one Hezbollah unit focused on fighting IDF infantry while another sought to destroy or disable tanks. Away from the border, particularly near main roads, other Hezbollah fighters with extensive training in weapon use (including ATGMs) sought to disable or destroy IDF High Mobility Multi-Purpose Wheeled Vehicles (HMMWVs) and tanks from standoff distances. They had to travel to their fighting areas, but their weapons were cached near where they expected to operate. These fighters sought to slow IDF manoeuvre and to cause casualties using surprise and hit-and- run tactics.

Hezbollah deployed their tank-killer teams in a thin but effective defensive scheme, protecting the villages where the organisation's Shiite members reside, where their short-range rockets were positioned and where command infrastructure and logistics support was set up. An estimated

500 to 600 members of their roughly 4,000-strong Hezbollah fighting strength in South Lebanon were divided into tank-killer teams of 5 or 6, each armed with 5–8 anti-tank missiles, with further supplies stored in small, fortified, well-camouflaged bunkers and basements, built to withstand Israeli air attacks.

Hezbollah also had a rocket force with the capability to conduct indirect-fire tasks into Israel. It declared that it sought to keep a regular and consistent rate of fire from its rocket force into Israel. Hezbollah personnel who worked with rockets and missiles received specialised training and operated in areas where they could hide from the IAF and where Israeli infantry could not move freely. Table 3 shows the broad array of Hezbollah rockets in Lebanon. Other Hezbollah weapon systems are shown in Table 4.

Table 3: Hezbollah Rockets, 2006

Type	Range (km)	Payload (kg)	Quantity
Short range:	7–40	7	13,000
107-mm *Katyusha*			
122-mm *Katyusha*			
122-mm Extended Range *Katyusha*			
240-mm *Katyusha*			
Intermediate range:	45–70	50–175	~1,000
240-mm *Fadjr-3*			
330-mm *Fadjr-5*			
220-mm *Urgan*			
302-mm *Khaibar-1*			
Long range:	200	400–600	Dozens
610-mm *Zelzal-2*			

Table 4: Other Hezbollah Weapons

Type and Name	Maximum Range (km)
Anti-ship missiles	
C-701	15
C-802 *Noor*	120
Unmanned aerial vehicles	
Ababil	NA
Antitank guided missiles	
AT-13 *Metis-M*	2
AT-4 *Spigot*	2
AT-3 *Sagger*	3
TOW	3.75
AT-5 *Spandrel*	4
AT-14 *Kornet-E*	5

The main characteristics of the rocket weaponry is at Table 5.

Table 5: Hezbollah Rocket Weaponry: Characteristics

Rocket	Calibre (mm)	Length (m)	Weight (kg)	Warhead Weight	Range (m) Min - Max	Remarks
Chinese Rockets						
Type 63 (*Fadjr*-1)	107	0.84-0.92	18.8	5	8,500	12-barrel launcher, towed, mounted on jeep or single launcher, portable
The Grad Series						
9M22U	122	3.226	66.2	19.4	1,500–20,389	BM-21 launcher with 40 barrels, and launchers with 12 or 36 barrels, and even portable single-barrel launchers
9M22M	122	2.870	66.0	18.4	1,500–20,000	
9M2B	122	1.905	45.8	19.4	2,500–10,800	Used by special forces
9M217	122		70	25	30,000	
9M218	122		70	25	40,000	
9M521	122		70	21	37,500	
Syrian Launchers						
220 mm.	220					A version of the *Ouragan*
302 mm.	302					Syrian version of Chinese WS-1
Iranian Launchers						
Fadjr-3	240	5.2	407	90	17,000–43,000	12 barrels on a truck
Fadjr-5	333	6.485	915	175	75,000	4 barrels on a truck
Falaq-1	240		111	50	10,000	4 barrels on a jeep
Falaq-2	333		255	120	10,800	1 barrel on a jeep
Zelzal-2	610	8.46	3400	600	210,000	Track on a truck
Other weapons						
Ouragan BM 9P 140 Rocket: 9M27F	220	4.8–5.1, according to type	280	100	10,000–35,000	Launcher—*Zil* 135 vehicle carrying 16 barrels with various types of rockets; apparently sold to Syria
WS-1	302	4.737	524	150	40,000–100,000	Made in China, possibly sold to Iran
WS-1B	302	6.375	725	150	60,000–180,000	Made in China
BM 9A52*Smerch*	300	7.6	800	120-130	20,000–70,000/ 90,000	12-barrel launcher

The main method of the IDF, and particularly the air force, to deal with the problem of rocket launches was to hit the launchers. The ideal situation is, of course, to hit the launcher prior to the launch. However, chances of success are slim, due to the launchers' low signature in the field and the difficulty of tracking them. The problem is less acute with regard to heavy rockets transported on heavy vehicles, which are easier to trace when they leave their hides. The problem is more serious when the launcher is a single barrel, transported on a motorcycle or a donkey, or concealed in a small bunker in an area covered with thick vegetation.

On the other hand, as soon as a launch has occurred it is easier to identify the launcher and pinpoint its precise location. The difficulty lies in completing the process of pinpointing and directing an aircraft to strike the launcher. This difficulty is illustrated by the attempt of the Americans to hit Iraq's Scud launchers during the Gulf War. Despite the launches being observed from distances of hundreds of kilometres the American war planes did not manage to hit a single launcher.

In southern Lebanon, distances do not pose such a serious problem, although a mobile launcher can still disappear from the field within a few seconds, particularly in a built-up or forested area. Thus, at least with regard to medium and heavy launchers, Israel's air force achieved highly impressive successes. These results were only achieved by virtue of the ability to complete the pinpointing process, connecting the attacker with the target so that the attacker reached the target before the launcher could vanish. This is naturally more difficult when dealing with a very large number of light launchers, as used by Hezbollah from the border area.

The technical data of the anti-tank missiles in the conflict arena are at Table 6.

Table 6: Hezbollah Anti-Tank Missiles

System	Range (metres)	Penetration (mm)	Guidance System (Manual/Laser/Wire)
Kornet AT–14	3,500	1,100–1,200	Laser
Kornet AT–5	75	800	Wire
Metis-M AT–13	1,500	460–850	Wire
Sagger AT–3	3,000	200	Wire
Fagot AT–4	2,000	400	Wire
Milan	2,000	352	Wire
TOW	3,700	800	Wire
RPG–29	460	750	Manual
RPG–7	500	3300	Manual

Countdown to War

The Israel Defence Forces had proposed a list of political goals to the government, which were presented to the prime minister and the cabinet on the night of July 12. These were:

1. To distance Hezbollah from the border with Israel.
2. To strike a significant blow against Hezbollah's military capability and status, and thereby put an end to terrorism originating from Lebanon.
3. To strengthen deterrence vis-à-vis Hezbollah and the entire region.
4. To correct the prevailing system in Lebanon, based on an effective enforcement mechanism that is supported by international involvement (this was later changed to "have the Lebanese government use the Lebanese army to impose its sovereignty over its entire territory").
5. To foster appropriate conditions for freeing the kidnapped IDF soldiers.
6. To accomplish these ends while keeping Syria out of the war.

The concept was designed by the IDF to be a platform proposed by the military to the political leadership (because the political leadership has long refrained from defining goals to the army), from which the campaign's goals are to be derived. Notably absent from the strategic purpose was any reference to Israel's home front.

Definition of the objectives changed during the fighting, in an effort to adapt them to the emerging situation. More importantly, however, statements by political figures, and sometimes also by senior military officers, employed careless and populist language. These statements created expectations among the public that did not match the discourse between the military and the civilian leadership. In addition, the goals ignored one of the fundamentals of Israel's security doctrine: any war initiated by Israel should have a defined and short timetable.

The political goals were translated into a list of missions for the operational headquarters. These amounted to extensive strikes by the air force against Hezbollah deep within Lebanon while isolating Lebanon from Syria, together with a series of ground operations in the Northern Command's theatre that would not drag the IDF into implementing its entire ground operations plan for southern Lebanon. The prevention of short range Katyusha rocket fire appeared later on the list of operational goals, after the military command fully realised its significance. What all these formulations had in common, from those made by the tactical command level to those by the political leadership, were the lack of simplicity and transparency necessary to make intentions clear.

THE AIR CAMPAIGN

The Air War

During meetings on July 12, the Israeli government decided to execute a bombing campaign to knock out Hezbollah's *Fajr* intermediate-range rockets (Operation *Specific Weight*), shut down the runways of the Beirut Rafiq Hariri International Airport, interdict the Beirut-Damascus highway, and attack the *al-Manar* television station. General Halutz, who had advocated an even broader attack that included the Lebanese electric grid, believed that the IDF had to respond vigorously and rapidly as he felt that "Israel had a limited margin of time, two to three days at most, before the international community intervened."

Clearly, air strikes were central to a plan that its designers assumed would damage Hezbollah, put pressure the Lebanese government to control Hezbollah, result in the release of the captured soldiers, and strengthen Israel's military deterrent. Furthermore, there was little appetite among civilian ministers for a large-scale ground campaign.

Prime Minister Olmert also appeared to assume that the decisive air campaign would force Hezbollah to sue for a ceasefire after only a few days, "during which time Israel would weather Katyusha fire". When Prime Minister Olmert talked to U.S. Secretary of State Condoleezza Rice on 12 July, she "gave a green light" to the Israeli strike plans. Secretary Rice also "brought up two American non-go's regarding the Israeli operation: Siniora must not be hurt and the civilian infrastructure must not be bombed." Prime Minister Olmert agreed to these demands. The United States viewed the Siniora government as key to future Lebanese stability and did not want to see it toppled as the result of Israeli military action. General Halutz was likely responsible for the prime minister's optimism.

The air force put its plan into operation on the night of 13 July. Within 35 minutes, the vast majority of Hezbollah's array of long range rockets and a large portion of the medium range rocket launchers were hit. In the course of the fighting, the air force destroyed all the medium range launchers from which rockets were actually launched. The IAF also blockaded Lebanese airspace, and the Israeli Navy blockaded Lebanese ports. Hezbollah responded to these attacks with an intense barrage of *Katyusha* rockets aimed at Israeli border settlements, and, for the first time, it fired rockets at Haifa, an Israeli city, 30 kilometres from the Lebanese border.

On 14 July, senior Israeli cabinet members met and approved IDF plans to bomb Dahiye, the southern Beirut suburb that housed Hezbollah's headquarters and Secretary-General Nasrallah's private residence. Proponents of the attack believed it would deliver a painful and surgical blow to Hezbollah's strength and honour. A minority at the meeting disagreed as an attack on Dahiye presaged all-out war on Hezbollah. The IAF began striking Dahiye on the evening of 14 July, and the suburb was transformed into a sea of rubble. Events would soon prove the sceptics correct.

In the coming weeks, the IAF stepped up its air attacks, striking Hezbollah command posts, bridges, traffic intersections, ammunition caches, and rocket launchers in southern Lebanon. Convoys suspected of carrying munitions between Syria and Lebanon were also struck. Artillery and naval bombardments were used to attack targets in Lebanon. Air attacks continued until the conclusion of the war on 14 August. The scale of air effort was enormous: During the war the IAF's fighters and helicopters carried out about 19,000 sorties, of which some 12,000 were fighter sorties in attack and support missions (an average of about 300 sorties a day). Attack and transport helicopters carried out some 4,200 additional sorties. Most of the air activity was directly aimed at Hezbollah. During the war, the IAF attacked about 7,000 targets, using about 19,000 bombs and about 2,000 missiles; approximately 35 percent of the ammunition used during the war was PGMs. In parallel to the kinetic operations, the IAF also operated in the information realm and dropped about 17.3 million leaflets.

The locations struck by the IAF during the war are shown at Map 5. The scope of the IAF's operations was unprecedented and absolutely disproportionate to Israel's past wars. All in all, there were more assault

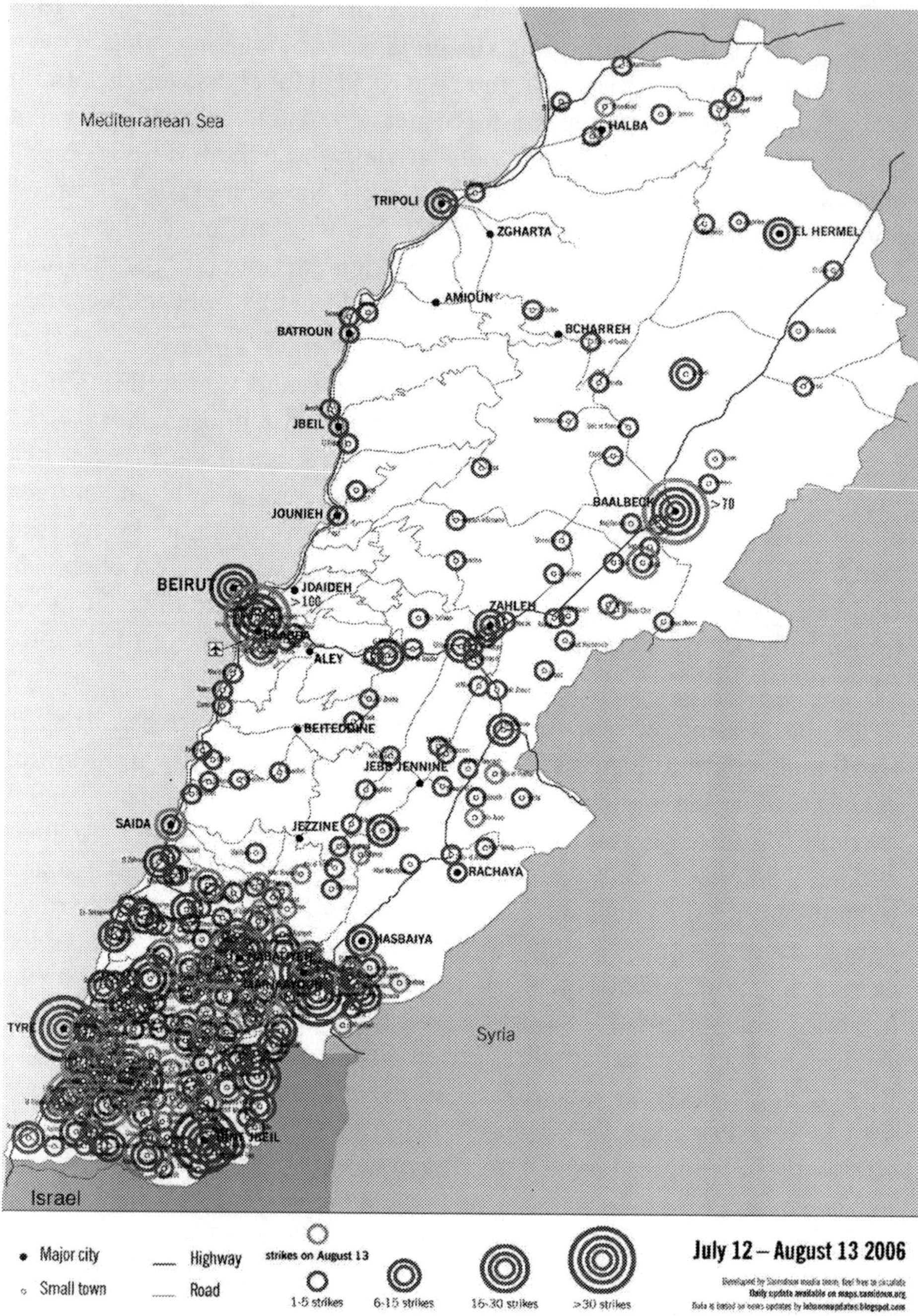

Map 5: Lebanese Targets Attacked by Israel

sorties and more flight hours than during the Yom Kippur War. Additionally, the Israeli Army fired 150,000 rounds (of 155-mm rounds and rockets), and the Israeli Navy fired more than 2,500 rounds. By 16 July 16, the IDF literally ran out of targets, having battered all 83 objectives on Northern Command's initial target list.

Israeli leaders had many valid reasons to want to use airpower:

(a) An airpower-centric approach best countered the enemy's strengths, particularly given how embedded Hezbollah was in Lebanese civil society and how much it had built up its basic capabilities north of the Litani River (and thus out of the reach of Israeli ground forces).

(b) The existing conception of conventional ground combat, attrition, and occupation prevalent in the IDF was out of sync with either the nature of the enemy or the level of commitment Israeli leaders (and, in their view, the Israeli public) were willing to make.

(c) The airpower decision was made easier by the reality that the ground forces were not prepared to mount the very campaign they were promoting.

The IAF enjoyed much more success in targeting Hezbollah's intermediate- and long-range rockets than in targeting its short-range arsenal. The IAF had intelligence, provided by the General Security Service, the *Mossad*, and Israeli Military Intelligence, on the long-range launchers, and it also had existing plans for attacking them.

During the war, the IAF adapted its techniques in order to find and destroy intermediate- and long-range launchers. These included using overhead sensors, special forces, and UAVs to both locate and track launchers and their crews and to carry out air strikes designed to destroy them. Intelligence, surveillance, and reconnaissance (ISR), particularly from UAVs, was very important in this effort. Nevertheless, throughout the conflict, Hezbollah was able to launch rockets into Israeli territory, launching an average of 90–150 attacks a day. Most of these attacks involved short-range *Katyushas* that the IAF was not able to find with air ISR platforms. The continual rain of Hezbollah rockets into Israel shocked the Israeli population and undermined the image of the IDF as an effective military force.

Quite simply, the IAF was unable to strike the short-range *Katyusha* alignment in a way that would limit the attacks on the Israeli home front.

In fact, the IAF had reached this assessment of its own capability in this area even before the war. The issue confronting Israeli decisionmakers was how to stop the short-range rockets. The minutes of a meeting of the General Staff, on 4 August, show that there was a growing recognition that standoff fires would not stop the short-range rockets. The head of the Intelligence Branch, with support from the head of the Research Division, opined that the only way of clearing the *Katyusha* rockets was with a significant ground operation. This was the course that was eventually adopted, with very mixed results.

The scale of the Israeli air attack surprised observers both inside and outside the Middle East. The international community denounced Israel for attacking Lebanon's infrastructure. Despite the air attack, however, Hezbollah was able to surprise the IDF in return. For example, on 14 July, Hezbollah hit the *Hanit*, an Israeli Sa'ar 5—class corvette—one of Israel's most advanced ships—with an Iranian-made C-802 *Noor* missile. The Israelis were not even aware that Hezbollah possessed this kind of missile. The ship's crew, not expecting to be attacked, had turned off its Barak antimissile system.

Use of Airpower

The air force operated in two different theatres: first, the air force was given command authority over the area stretching from the Litani River northward (the deep theatre of operations). In the second theatre, south of the Litani, the air force was tasked to support the Northern Command's operations and was controlled by the Command's HQ. That included independent air missions serving the Northern Command's operations, as well as close support for the ground forces. The deep theatre of operations, namely, the missions and objectives that were to be achieved north of the Litani River included:

- *Striking the rocket launch capability*. Air force attacks were aimed at damaging Hezbollah's launching capabilities. Naturally mostly medium and longer-range rocket were deployed in this arena and the attacks on them were very successful. The short-range rockets deployed in the closer areas, however, posed a different challenge because of their low signature and great number, and the achievements in the attacks against them were insignificant. Some medium range rockets were launched from the area of Tyre that falls under the

Northern Command's responsibility. Nevertheless, the air force was given the authority to operate independently against them and did so successfully.

- *Destroying Hezbollah's organisational and operational infrastructures*. From the first day of the fighting the air force tried to impair Hezbollah's organisational and operational infrastructures deep in this arena. Control centres, communications systems, and the Dahiya quarter that hosted the Hezbollah HQ indeed were hit and suffered significant damage; apparently the greatest damages were inflicted on Hezbollah's organisational infrastructures and in the Dahiya quarter.
- *Isolating the war arena*. The air force operated to isolate the fighting arena by hitting the Lebanese transportation infrastructure, which likely contributed to the overall pressure on the Lebanese government.
- *Damaging Lebanese national infrastructures*. The air force was limited in damaging Lebanon's national infrastructures due to a government constraint imposed from the outset of the fighting.

Command of the Deep Theatre of Operations

This is probably the first time the air force was given overall authority for a geographical theatre. In order to apply this authority, the air force had to implement a full command and control cycle. This included all the relevant processes involved, from receipt of the orders from the chief of staff, through operational planning, issuing command orders and sub-missions, controlling the implementation by the forces, and finally, reviewing achievement of the objectives and the missions. As part of this process, the theatre command had to optimise force operation by identifying the best composition of the force for achieving the missions. This is the essence of integrated force operation. During the war, the air force appears to have struggled to implement this authority fully, and thus in effect operated more as a firepower and targets contractor. This may be the result of the operational culture of the air force and the manner in which historically it perceives its role in warfare. Developing the air force's capability to serve as an effective central command in a geographical operational combat theatre requires its internalising the different needs and processes and its implementing all the components of force build-up: training officers, developing doctrine, exercises, organisation, and development of weapon systems. Given the challenges of future wars, whereby the air force will be called on to carry out similar missions, including command responsibility for other theatres of war, it will be required to generate such a process as quickly as possible in order to enhance the effectiveness of its theatre command.

Air Force Support to the Northern Command Operations

The air force deployed a control facility at the Northern Command HQ to control airpower operations in the command's theatre according to its tasking and priorities. In practice, the link between this control facility and the Northern Command HQ failed to operate effectively. In addition, the air strikes against the short-range rocket system were unsuccessful, mainly due to the fact that the rocket launches did not have an adequate signature that enabled the air force to complete attack cycles i.e. the process of identifying the target, attacking the target, and examining the results of the attack.

The close air support proved inadequate. It was designed to enable commanders in the battlefield to direct attack helicopters and attack aircraft against specific targets, according to the battle needs and in real time. The use of air assets in the Northern Command theatre failed to achieve its goals. It seems that the ability to use close air support has declined in recent years, largely due to the degeneration of the liaison system that was established in the past between the air force and the ground forces. The air support system has for all intents and purposes been terminated.

A summary of Israeli air operations is given at Table 7.

Table 7: Israeli Air Operations

Total sorties	15,500
Combat sorties	10,000
Combat helicopter sorties	About 2,000
Reconnaissance flights	More than 1,300
Transport flights	About 1,200
Targets struck	7,000 plus
Types of targets struck	Headquarters, bases, rocket launchers (300), Hezbollah-associated structures (1800), Hezbollah-associated vehicles (270), bridges (350)

Comments

During the fighting, the air force operated at almost full capacity. It succeeded in accomplishing most of the goals assigned to it.

In addition, the air force carried out the following missions:

(a) Limited attacks on Lebanese ground targets and attacks on Hezbollah targets—these attacks were intended to affect Hezbollah's ability to continue and renew the fighting. The effectiveness of these attacks is unclear.

(b) It demolished the Dahiya neighbourhood in Beirut, a closed quarter used by Hezbollah as both a residence and an operational control area.

(c) It intercepted and shot down the *Ababil* UAVs that Hezbollah launched towards Israel.

(d) During the fighting, together with other IDF units operating various radar devices, the air force created a system for detecting rocket launchings in order to provide advance warning to the home front.

(e) During the war, it executed approximately 120 rescue missions, nearly half of them in enemy territory. Three hundred sixty wounded soldiers were rescued in these missions. It also parachuted supplies to IDF fighting units.

(f) In the later stages of the fighting, the air force began operations against Katyusha deployment. The effectiveness of these attacks was limited, and this activity did not alter the rate of Katyusha fire against Israel.

To attain these achievements, the air force consumed a large quantity of resources:

(a) The total number of sorties during the fighting was only slightly fewer than in the Yom Kippur War.

(b) The total number of attack missions flown during the fighting was greater than in the Yom Kippur War.

(c) The total number of combat helicopter missions flown was double the number flown in the first Lebanon war, Operation *Accountability*, and Operation *Grapes of Wrath* combined.

(d) The air force depleted its supply of certain types of armaments, resulting in a need for immediate stocks from overseas.

The marginal effectiveness of the air force combat missions declined steeply as the fighting progressed, mostly because of the unlikely ratio of the number of targets with any value whatsoever (which dropped sharply) to the forces available to and operated by designers of the aerial combat.

To critics of airpower, Israel's 2006 war with Hezbollah exposed the fallacy that targeting centres of gravity, such as population, command and control, and infrastructure could coerce the adversary into surrendering, and that airpower could obviate the need for land forces and independently win wars. Given Israel's unexpected challenges in waging the Lebanon war, airpower and then Chief of Staff Dan Halutz, seen as the overzealous proponent of airpower, became easy targets in after-action reports, criticism that ultimately led to Halutz's resignation and replacement by Gaby Ashkenazi, an infantry officer.

In the use of airpower, there were three weaknesses in the Israeli strategy:

(a) The Israeli leadership's faith in airpower as an antiseptic, low-casualty answer for modern warfare clouded the possibility of other strategies that may have been more effective in achieving its objectives.

(b) The leadership suffered from the classic "fighting the last war" mentality, internalising the lessons from the Kosovo military campaign, where airpower was successful, and applying it to an incongruous environment.

(c) Airpower was ultimately counterproductive against an asymmetric adversary such as Hezbollah. By launching mobile *katyusha* rockets from holy sites and schools, Hezbollah virtually ensured that Israel would inflict civilian casualties; through its strategic use of the media, Hezbollah used the collateral damage to intensify support for its ideology and recruitment. In this asymmetric environment, airpower and perhaps military force more generally may be limited in their effectiveness. Only a comprehensive strategy that integrates airpower and military force into a broader political strategy will ultimately bring this type of adversary to its knees.

While airpower did not achieve Israel's strategic objectives—the two soldiers remain unreturned and Hezbollah was still launching 100 rockets a day into Israel up until the tenuous UN-sponsored cease-fire—it also was not an abject failure. The IDF, operating primarily through its air assets, is thought to have eliminated about 500 of Hezbollah's most advanced fighters, and forced many of the others to evacuate the areas south of the Litani River. Use of airpower did destroy about half of the unused longer-range rockets, and much of Lebanon's infrastructure, used to resupply Hezbollah, was destroyed. After the war, Hezbollah leader Hassan Nasrallah indicated that had he understood the degree to which Israel would retaliate, he may have been more cautious about the capture of two Israeli soldiers in the first place. Thus, the IDF may have encountered challenges but may also have fought defiantly enough to create a deterrent for future Hezbollah aggression.

Given the limited effects of airpower against asymmetric adversaries, and the domestically and internationally unpopular prospect of using ground forces against Hezbollah, what were Israel's strategic options? The Israeli government could not stand by and appear to do nothing when rockets were falling on Israeli towns and soldiers were being captured. Moreover, the government, new to office and seeking to fill the large shoes left by General Sharon, was right to assert its right of self-defence and retaliate in some manner. While airpower offered a way to demonstrate leadership resolve and appeal to society's interest in doing something, and without the need to mount legislative and civilian support for the otherwise riskier strategy of using ground troops, it clearly faced challenges in the execution. What are the lessons to draw from those challenges?

The first lesson, based on this analysis, would be to suggest caution when applying anything but contextualised lessons from the last war. Certainly, no two wars are the same, but some are more similar than others. Noting the strategic context—conventional, asymmetric, etc.—is key to understanding how best to match the strategy to the adversary. By thinking not just about whether a particular approach worked, but by placing that approach in a particular context and then evaluating its utility, leaders may be better able to avoid the pathology of fighting a war that happens to be incongruent with their immediate context.

A second lesson is perhaps not that airpower is a categorical failure, but that it does not promise the antiseptic elixir that some leaders are seeking. If leaders are serious about providing security, they must identify their strategic objectives and match them with appropriate and realistic instruments and be willing to use those instruments even at the risk of incurring casualties. Conflicts such as the Gulf War and Kosovo may have given the impression that high precision stand-off weapons can deliver victory with few casualties, but these may have been the anomalies. The very nature of a war makes bloodshed likely. While acting within the bounds of proportionality, a state's leadership's business is to provide for their state's security and win wars; "kind-heartedness" is not always the best way to achieve that goal.

Third, the outcome of a conventional military against an asymmetric adversary may show that not just airpower, but military force in general may have limited effectiveness in this type of unconventional environment. Given the way opponents use casualties as political theatre for generating support, the use of military force, which inevitably leads to casualties, will likely only invigorate a resistance that is founded more on an ideology than on the material power that fuels conventional militaries. Since the opposition is as much ideological as military, then it is not clear that only the use of force—land, air, or some combination thereof—will itself bring the adversary to its knees. Rather, the use of force should be integrated within a broader political strategy designed to collapse support for the adversary.

In these asymmetric settings, much of the conflict may play out in the battlefield of the media. The centres of gravity against asymmetric adversaries may not be their infrastructure and command and control nodes, which are severely lacking compared to regular armies. Lacking high-value assets, the centres of gravity for asymmetric adversaries may become their citizens' political will. And as the case of the Lebanon war and the draw for foreign fighters and civilians shows, "citizens" may not mean the citizens of that particular state, but the individuals who are inclined in a similar ideological way, whether they live in Somalia, Syria, Lebanon, or Egypt. The public relations battle therefore may not be limited to information operations (IO) in the immediate area of operations, in this case Lebanon, but across boundaries, targeting individuals that may be sympathetic to the cause taking place on foreign lands. Any information operations strategy, whether jamming radio transmissions of the adversary or disseminating information favourable to friendly forces, must therefore be deployed not just locally but on a more widespread basis, to include potential foreign fighters.

Moreover, to the extent that asymmetric battles may be part of a broader ideological struggle, any wartime IO strategies must be combined with wider-ranging political strategies. Until states can make advances on the battlefield of public relations, they are unlikely to see decisive victories on the battlefield of tanks, missiles, and planes.

THE GROUND CAMPAIGN

The War Unfolds

The IDF responded within two hours, to the abductions of its soldiers, sending a platoon-sized *Nahal* force and a *Merkava* tank from the 7th Armoured Brigade across the border in a retaliatory attack on Hezbollah's nearest posts and to capture a vantage point on Giv'at Hadegel, a nearby hill on the Lebanese side (site of a Hezbollah post), and to take control of the exit roads from the village of Ita a-Sha'ab on the possibility that the abductors were still there. The resources available to the 91st Division Commander were limited, and, given the amount of time that had passed since the abduction, this action was more of a retaliatory attack on nearby Hezbollah positions than a pursuit of the abductors. During this incursion, the *Merkava* tank was destroyed by a large IED when it attempted to run over a Hezbollah hut, and the four members of the tank's crew were killed. An additional *Nahal* force was sent to prevent Hezbollah from taking the bodies, but Hezbollah attacked this force with mortar fire, killing another IDF soldier.

At the time of the abduction, Hezbollah also attacked Israeli military outposts and the towns of Shlomi and Sha'ba Farms with rockets, as an attempt to divert Israeli attention during the kidnapping. Hamas and other groups were also launching rockets at Israel. The IDF was also involved at the time in large-scale operations in Gaza to attempt to recover kidnapped Israeli soldier, Corporal Gilad Shalit. The Hezbollah and Shalit abductions were viewed by Israeli leaders as part of a pattern of terrorist activity that would only get worse if it was not dealt with aggressively. On 12 July, the IDF further responded to the Hezbollah abductions with pre-planned air strikes against 17 Hezbollah locations in Lebanon and against three bridges that spanned the Litani River. The attacks on bridges were to prevent the movement of the abducted soldiers out of southern Lebanon.

Israeli political and military leaders met to discuss the abduction and rocket attacks and agreed that Israel needed to respond with military force. However, both the political and the military leadership expressed reluctance to send a large ground force into Lebanon, preferring instead to rely on airstrikes and limited ground raids on towns of symbolic importance. This decision meant that the on-the-shelf plan for a war in southern Lebanon—Operation *Sky Water*—was not executed. This plan called for a massive Israeli Army sweep to isolate the southern part of Lebanon from northern sources of supply, and then eradicate the Hezbollah in the sealed off area. An alternative plan—Operation *Ice Breaker*—based on standoff fire and limited cross-border raids was also not fully put into action. As late as 18 July, General Halutz, the IDF chief of staff, stated that here is no point planning a ground operation. Initially, Israeli leaders also decided against calling up reserves.

Israel's Strategy

At the beginning of the conflict in Lebanon, the IDF had very limited goals. The 12 July communiqué, issued after the emergency meeting of the Israeli Security Cabinet, framed the initial Israeli response to the soldiers' abductions. It stated that Israel viewed the sovereign Lebanese Government as responsible for the action that originated on its soil and for the return of the abducted soldiers to Israel. It demanded that the Lebanese Government implement UN Security Council Resolution 1559. It also stated that Israel will respond aggressively and harshly to those who carried out, and are responsible for the action, and will work to foil actions and efforts directed against it. Israel would respond with the necessary severity to this act of aggression.

The lack of significant military experience among the senior political figures in the Israeli Security Cabinet hampered development of a coherent strategy. Compared with past Israeli political leaders who were career military officers, these three had little experience working with senior military officers or developing broad military strategy prior to their political careers. Also, the military, and particularly General Halutz, did little to compensate for the lack of expertise among Israeli politicians. This became apparent as the war unfolded. Halutz did not alert the political leadership to the serious shortcomings in the preparedness and the fitness of the armed forces for an extensive ground operation, if that became necessary. In addition, he did not clarify that the military assessments and analyses indicated that there was a high probability that a military strike against Hezbollah would make a ground operation necessary. The military objectives were mainly focused on deterrence.

A 12 July order framed how the IDF would prosecute operations in Lebanon in the coming weeks. The operational order reflected the military's understanding of the specific list of missions assigned to them. It instructed the IDF to destroy Hezbollah's long-range rocket launchers and to damage the organisation's launch capability, attack its soldiers, attack its command infrastructure, strike its symbols and assets, and destroy Hezbollah infrastructures in the proximity of the Israeli border in order to establish a special security zone. At the same time, the IDF was instructed to set up an aerial and naval blockade to prevent Syria and Iran from supplying arms to Hezbollah.

On 19 July, Israel's strategy to reach its desired political end state were determined by the Ministerial Committee on National Security Affairs. It stated that the principles for the political solution of the crisis, in the Lebanese theatre will be:

(a) Release of the abducted soldiers and returning them to Israel unconditionally;

(b) Stopping of the firing of missiles and rockets against the residents of the State of Israel and against Israeli targets;

(c) Full and complete application of Resolution 1559 of the United Nations, including disarming all of the armed militias, applying the sovereignty of the Government of Lebanon to its entire territory and deployment of the Lebanese Army along the border with Israel.

This strategy required the Lebanese government to do something it clearly lacked the ability to do, regardless of its inclinations. The ability of the IDF to employ military force to achieve these political objectives would soon be tested.

The Initial Ground Raids

In keeping with the new doctrine, Chief of the IDF General Staff, Dan Halutz had no intention of implementing a ground invasion plan and activating IDF reserve forces. Days into the war, he still felt the air campaign would succeed. However, Halutz was under pressure from army commanders to initiate a reserve call-up in the event a full-scale ground invasion became necessary. A compromise was reached that allowed the regular army to carry out limited battalion- and brigade-size raids into Lebanon. These raids were not designed to destroy Hezbollah or its rockets but to craft a *consciousness of victory* for the Israelis and a *cognitive perception of defeat* for Hezbollah though the air campaign could not destroy the *Katyushas* (falling on northern Israel at a rate of approximately 100 a day).

On 17 July 2006, IDF ground forces, led by Special Forces groups, opened a 60-kilometre front in southern Lebanon, stretching from the Mediterranean coast to the Lebanese border town of Maroun al-Ras. Under the cover of darkness and air and artillery fire, 300 Israeli soldiers, supported by 12 *Merkava* tanks, crossed into Lebanon and ascended to the hilltop town of Maroon al-Ras en route to Bint J'Beil, a large town north of Maroun al-Ras. Seizing Maroun al-Ras and its surrounding heights would provide the IDF with secure lines of communication to sustain a large raid into Bint J'Beil and its surrounding hills and villages. Control of the Maroun al-Ras area would also deny Hezbollah tactically important high ground and disrupt rocket teams operating in the area.

Early into the operation, the advancing Israeli commandos became entangled in heavy fighting along the freshly ploughed hilltops that concealed Hezbollah bunkers. Hezbollah fighters, manoeuvring in the dark and through their tunnels, began encircling the commandos, forcing the vanguard of the Israeli invasion to slow its advance to await reinforcements. Tanks and engineer vehicles brought from the rear to prevent the encirclement struggled to engage the Hezbollah fighters as they encountered roads lined with anti-tank mines and IEDs that shredded the tracks of the Israeli tanks, clogging the avenues of approach into Maroun al-Ras.

Hezbollah fighters vigorously resisted the Israeli incursions. Their determination and strength stunned Israel, which, despite its continuous bombardment of Hezbollah positions and lines of communications, had not broken the Hezbollah capability or will to resist. Israeli soldiers were also unprepared for the size and strength of the defence. They entered Maroun al-Raas expecting to confront an enemy that was lightly armed; instead, they encountered a well-prepared and motivated enemy dug into a well-equipped network of tunnels. Often, the Israelis did not even know where the enemy bunkers were, until they were right on top of them, leading to dozens of fierce close-quarter firefights.

By 24 July, elements of the Golani Brigade and the 7th Armoured Brigade had established over-watch positions around Bint Jbeil. On 25 July, the 35th Paratrooper Brigade began moving northwest of the town in an attempt to establish a blocking position. The same day, the 91st Division Commander, Brigadier General Gal Hirsch, announced to the press that his forces were in control of Bint Jbeil. This, however, was not the case. As Hezbollah rockets continued to rain down on Israel and kill Israeli citizens, Halutz ordered the commander of IDF northern forces, Lieutenant General Udi Adam, to attack the town. Hezbollah Secretary-General Nasrallah had delivered his well-known victory speech in Bint Jbeil after the 2000 Israeli withdrawal from Lebanon. Halutz asserted that capturing the town would prove symbolic and create a *spectacle of victory* designed to effect *the cognitive perception* of Hezbollah. In the end, however, the battle for Bint Jbeil would have a greater effect on the Israeli public's perception of the IDF's professionalism and judgment.

After consolidating its control over Maroun al-Ras and its surrounding hills, the IDF prepared to press its advance further north to Bint J'beil. Slowly, under the cover of air and artillery fire, the Israelis tightened the noose around the village. From the southeast, the Golani Brigades seized tactically important hills that overlook the Hezbollah base of operations, while paratroopers secured the hills in southwest. Directly south of the town, 7th Armoured Brigade set-up over-watch positions. From their hilltop redoubts, the IDF launched probing attacks into the town to test its defences. The defenders responded ferociously, pushing back the initial attempts to enter the town. Attempts to penetrate the town defences with armoured vehicles also failed, as two *Merkava* IV tanks struck large IEDs, disabling them.

Halutz ordered Adam to conquer Bint Jbeil with just one battalion. Adam was infuriated and stated that the *casbah* (old quarter) of the town alone contained more than 5,000 houses. His protests were to no avail and, around 0500 hours on 26 July, after an intense artillery bombardment of the town, the 51st Battalion of the Golani Brigade assaulted Bint Jbeil from the east. (See Map 6). Many of the soldiers had little to no sleep over the previous three days of combat. The exhausted Israeli infantrymen advanced down the town's maze-like roads towards the centre market, where a company-sized force of Hezbollah fighters waited. The town was eerily quiet during the advance, as Hezbollah waited for its enemies to enter deeper into its defences. The few remaining townspeople hid in their

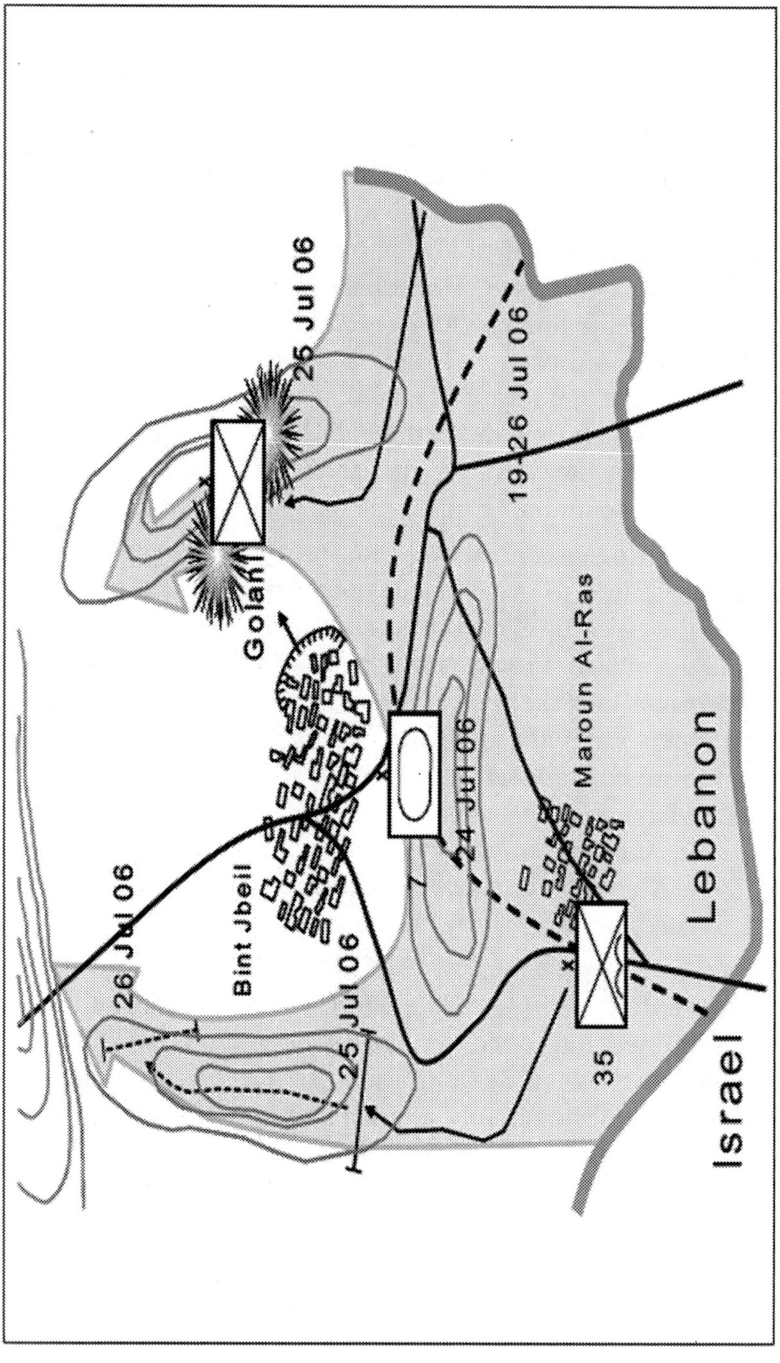

Map 6: The Battle of Bint Jbeil

basements and local shelters. Most people, however, had left the town in the hours leading up to the operations after Israeli radio messages and leaflets warned them to evacuate.

The steady push into the town came to a halt near the centre market when a lone fighter emerged from the shadows, drawing Israeli fire. At 0530 hours, A and C Companies of the 51st Battalion ran headlong into a withering array of Hezbollah small arms, machine guns, RPGs, antitank missiles, mortars, and short-range rockets. Chaos quickly ensued; nearly 100 Hezbollah fighters converged on the fighting via rooftops and alleyways. Finding the Israelis exposed in the streets below, the militants unleashed streams of automatic weapons fire down on the soldiers.

In the initial firing, 30 soldiers of C Company, one-third of its total strength, were hit, as was the battalion's Deputy Commander, Major Roi Klein, who sacrificed himself to save his men by diving on a grenade. A Company also sustained five casualties. As the fighting intensified, Hezbollah squads manoeuvred onto their flanks and continued to engage with direct and indirect fire. For hours, the fight raged. A and C Companies continued to resist the violent attacks, as other companies from the 51st Battalion rushed forward to assist with the evacuation of dead and wounded. It would take all night to evacuate them. In all, nine soldiers died and 27 were wounded.

As news of the engagement and rising casualties trickled from the town, the Israelis ordered additional infantry companies to reinforce the stalled advance. Blackhawk helicopters also arrived to evacuate the wounded and provide additional firepower. But the Israelis were wary of using helicopters against Hezbollah. Pre-war intelligence had led them to believe that Hezbollah had acquired advanced shoulder-fired surface-to-air missiles, like the SA-18.

Soon, tanks from three Israeli brigades entered the fight, along with the Egoz unit from the Golani Brigade, an engineer battalion, and 101st Battalion of the Paratroop Brigade. Heavy close quarters fighting between the Golani brigades and the militants raged for two more days. On 28 July, Israeli paratroopers reinforced the assault and the entire central market district—scenes of the most intense fighting was blasted—with mortars and artillery. However, Hezbollah fighters continued to occupy Bint Jbeil. Even by the end of the war, the town was never entirely secured by the IDF.

For Israel, the casualties had a major effect on public support for the war. As Israeli causalities rose following the ground invasion, Israeli public support for the invasion plummeted. This deep fear of casualties also undermined military operations. Every casualty was reported to the Chief of Staff, and there was a case in which an entire battle was stopped because of one casualty.

Hezbollah surprised Israel with the intensity of its resistance at Bint J'beil. A central reason for Israel's inability to anticipate the strength of Hezbollah's defence was poor intelligence on the organisation and the terrain in southern Lebanon. These failures resulted in three problems for Israel before and during the battle:

(a) The slow predictable approach to the town on 24 July aided Hezbollah with determining the Israelis' direction of approach and intentions, enabling them to set up ambush points and IEDs along the route. Better intelligence on Hezbollah and its area of operations would have allowed the Israelis to advance more rapidly. Instead, commanders moved slowly to contact without knowledge of what was ahead of them.

(b) Israeli intelligence underestimated the quality and numbers of militants in the town. The troops were shocked that there were large numbers of militants in the town, especially ones proficient in tactical manoeuvre under fire.

(c) The IDF had little knowledge of Hezbollah's more advanced weaponry, including the Russian made AT-14 (*Kornet*) and RPG-29. These weapons were capable of defeating any Israeli armoured vehicle, including the *Merkava*.

While fighting raged in the towns and hills of southern Lebanon, Hezbollah launched an all-out assault on Israeli civilian and military communications networks. Hezbollah hackers shut down Israeli phone systems, electric grids, and IT systems periodically throughout the war. At the same time, they hacked into phone lines and eavesdropped on Israeli conversations, including those of Israeli soldiers, who, in many instances, gave away important tactical information on phone calls home. The hackers even cracked encrypted Israeli military communications, providing the militants with information on Israeli movements and intentions. Through electronic warfare, Hezbollah made life even more difficult in northern Israel and, at the same time, gained valuable, tactical intelligence on its enemies.

Taken aback by the ineffective air campaign and surprised by Hezbollah's stubborn resistance in Maroun al-Ras, Olmert and Halutz called up Israeli reserve forces on 21 July. The decision to call the reserves took key senior reserve officers, usually the first to be notified of a pending call-up, by surprise. The reserve call-up was handled chaotically—with the reserve 'tail' of logistical support lagging some 24–48 hours behind the deployment of reserve forces. Also, the call-up was not designed to assist the regular army in the massive ground invasion of southern Lebanon. Although it would allow Israel to amass forces along the border, the ground plan remained unchanged. There would be no determined effort to drive Hezbollah back across the Litani or destroy its rockets with a large-scale ground assault.

On the same day the IDF reserve forces were called to duty, Israel was forced to request an emergency resupply of precision-guided missiles from the US. In 10 days, the IAF had used up most of its high-tech munitions, and yet, this huge expenditure of weaponry did little to change Hezbollah's military logic or its fighting capability. Mossad had gathered information indicating that Hezbollah had not suffered a significant degradation in its military capabilities, and that the organisation might be able to carry on the conflict for several months.

For nearly two weeks, Israeli reservists had been mustering and massing on the Lebanese border, preparing to reinforce their comrades who were fighting in Lebanon. The roads and farm fields of northern Israel choked with tanks, soldiers, and supplies. The Israeli higher command hoped to use these forces to establish a buffer zone that would prevent Hezbollah from firing rockets into Israel or mounting cross-border raids. Israel, however, was unable to create this zone through its approach of air strikes and limited battalion to brigade-sized raids. Pressure was beginning to build within the General Staff to increase the size and scope of the ground assault. It was clear that, without a major ground campaign, the IDF could not stop the *Katyusha* rockets. However, General Halutz remained committed to the air war backed by limited ground raids.

Finally, on 5 August, Israeli political leadership decided to expand the ground war in hopes of pushing Hezbollah back from the northern Israeli border. To achieve their scaled-down objectives, Israel had to move quickly, as international and domestic pressure was rapidly mounting; the prospect of a ceasefire grew more and more likely with each passing day.

The Litani Offensive

Operation ***Changing Direction*** was meant to be a large, and broad ground operation, which would fundamentally alter the situation in Southern Lebanon. It was originally scheduled to begin on 9 August but was delayed by two days. The goals of the operation were essentially two-fold:

(a) Create conditions on the ground that would result in a UN Security Council resolution on the war favourable to Israel, by having IDF forces push toward the Litani River.

(b) Reduce the volume of rocket fire on Israel.

The offensive was Israel's last chance to free its northern border of Hezbollah before any impending ceasefire came into effect. It would be a bloody affair, and Israel pulled no punches, placing the lives of Lebanese civilians in even greater peril. In leaflets dropped by fighter planes across southern Lebanon, Israel warned that any vehicle of any kind traveling south of the Litani River will be bombed, on suspicion of transporting rockets, military equipment, and terrorists.

Planning for the offensive in southern Lebanon began on 3 August, on the directions of Defence Minister Peretz. The plan was approved by him, on 7 August, and by the Israeli Security Cabinet, on 9 August. Several preparatory moves for the envisioned operation were begun overnight on 8–9 August.

Ground operations until this point generally had been executed by brigades and smaller units and could best be characterised as raids. Israeli special operations forces were also involved, having conducted a number of raids into Lebanon. One such raid was a 5 August naval commando unit action in Tyre, in which 27 Hezbollah and Iranian Revolutionary Guard operatives were killed. Before this, Israeli special operations forces had conducted at least 17 operations inside Lebanon, including a 2 August action undertaken by *Sayeret Matkal* and *Shaldag* commandos on a Hezbollah headquarters facility in Baalbeck in which ten Hezbollah members were killed and five were captured.

Four Israeli divisions participated in the offensive:

(a) **91 Infantry Division** (Galilee Formation). It was responsible for the entire sector until 21 July, when it transferred the eastern sector to 162 Armoured Division. Its main area of fighting was in and around Bint Jbeil.

(b) **162 Armoured Division** (Steel Formation). It fought in the eastern sector from 21 July. Its two-brigade attack on al-Khiam ended on 25 July.

(c) **98 Paratroopers Division** (Fire Formation). It began operations in the central sector on 30 July.

(d) **366 Reserve Armoured Division** (Pillar of Fire Formation). It took over responsibility for the eastern sector from 162 Division on 4 August. It fought in the area of Marj Ayoun and al-Khiam between 8-10 August.

All four divisions primarily conducted battalion and brigade-sized raids against Hezbollah positions and rocket locations. It was not a coordinated Northern Command campaign to accomplish a collective objective linked to a strategic end state.

Operation ***Changing Direction*** began at 1700 hours on 11 August, even as final negotiations on the UN-brokered ceasefire were nearing a conclusion. It was the first large-scale IDF coordinated ground action of the war. Perhaps the most problematic aspect of the operation was the fact that, given the impending ceasefire, Prime Minister Olmert allotted only 60 hours for its completion. The original plan, presented by Major General Gadi Eizenkot, then head of IDF Operations Directorate, had envisioned a much longer campaign: The first stage—during which the forces would reach their positions—envisaged four days; the second stage of fighting was anticipated to take three to four weeks; and the third stage, to withdraw the troops would take one week.

Operation ***Changing Direction*** was a four-division operation. In broad outline, the plan envisioned:

(a) 91 Infantry Division pressing north.

(b) 162 Armoured Division crossing the Saluki River from the east and pushing north (where it would link up with 98 Paratroopers Division along the Litani River).

(c) 98 Paratroopers Division conducting a helicopter assault and moving to the Litani River in the direction of Tyre.

(d) 366 Reserve Armoured Division attacking Hezbollah forces north of Metula.

The scheme of manoeuvre for Operation *Changing Direction* is shown in

Map 7. The divisions' objectives and outcomes before the cessation of hostilities at 0800 hours on 14 August were:

91 Division. It was to sweep through the eastern sector of southern Lebanon, taking and holding key terrain to prevent rocket launches and conducting clearing and sweep operations. Its principal role was to serve as a reserve for the primary effort by 162 Division, which would come from the north. Part of 91 Division's mission was to complete the occupation of Bint Jbeil and Eita a-Sha'ab—objectives that it did not accomplish. The overall performance of the division had little effect on the outcome of the operation as the 98 Division failed to accomplish its mission.

162 Division. It constituted Northern Command's main effort in Operation *Changing Direction*. Its mission was to take up positions throughout the western sector of southern Lebanon. The division began operations to breach the Wadi Saluki on 9 August but stopped these activities when the operation was delayed. On 11 August, the division began clearing missions along the border. On 12 August, the division's 401 Armoured Brigade began offensive operations to cross Wadi Saluki. It was a risky operation as crossing the Saluki required the troops and tanks to climb a steep hill overlooked in every direction. Hezbollah knew that the only passage West was through the Saluki. At least 100 guerrillas took up positions with the most advanced anti-tank missile—the Russian-made *Kornet*—and waited. The division commander, aware of the risks, had positioned infantry from the Nahal Brigade near the villages of Andouriya and Farun to cover the armoured brigade's passage. A column of tanks from the 401 Armoured Brigade's 9th Battalion approaching a crossing was ambushed by a well-armed and well-prepared Hezbollah force.

The 9th Battalion was to be supported by the 931st *Nahal* Battalion, but coordination between the two units was poor, even though their respective brigade commanders were co-located. The 9th Battalion's troops were also inadequately trained. They did not use smoke canisters mounted on their tanks that would have made the tanks more difficult to target. The tank column called for artillery and air support, but Northern Command denied these requests because of concerns about the possibility of hitting nearby friendly forces. The battalion halted and failed to open the route across the Saluki. Twelve IDF soldiers were killed and 44 were wounded.

On 13 August, the 401 Brigade tried again to force a crossing to the

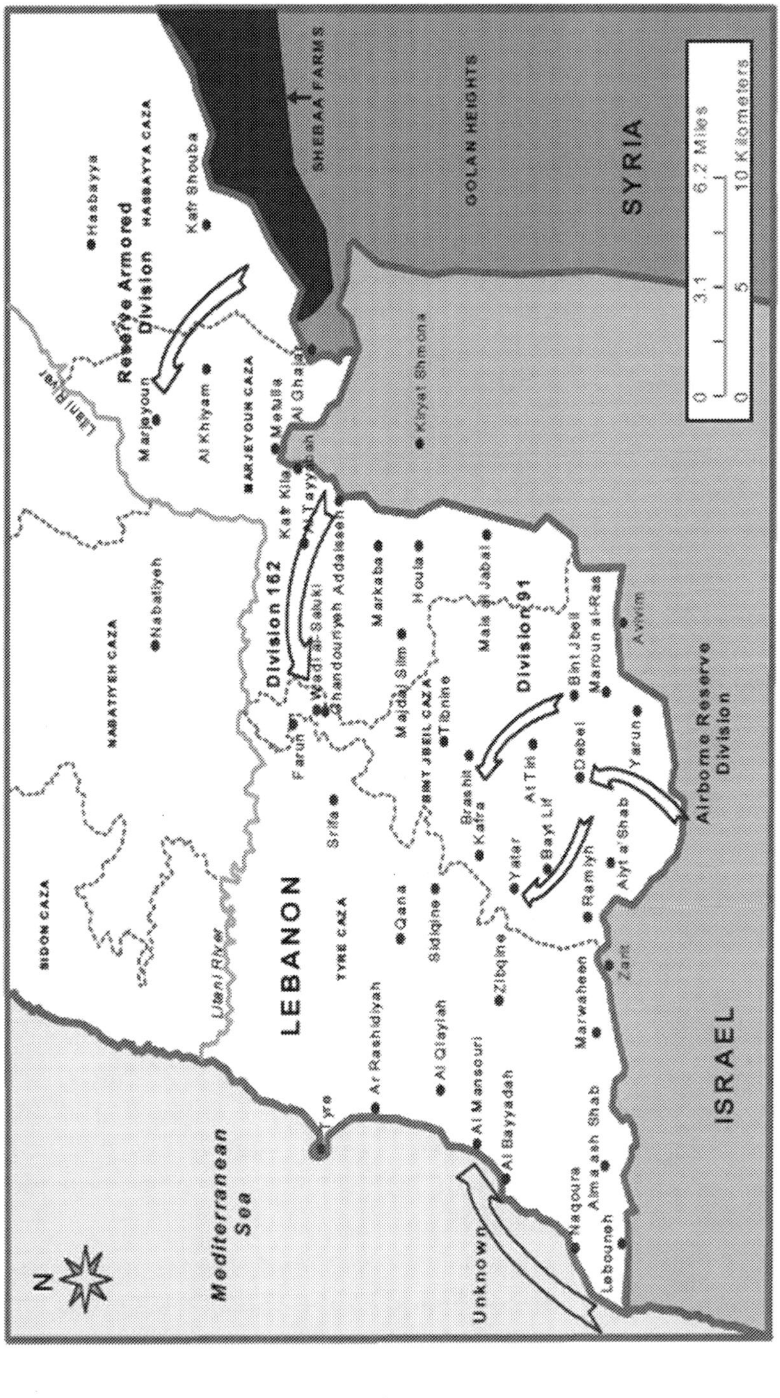

Map 7: Ground Scheme of Manoeuvre—Operation *Changing Direction*

west side of the Saluki. It had succeeded by 0300 hours, but the offensive was halted by Northern Command. The division did not accomplish its missions.

98 Division. IDF paratroopers in this division had begun executing operations on 8 August (prior to implementation of Operation *Changing Direction*) by seizing the village of Debel and holding houses along the edge of the village. Hezbollah attacked one of these houses with ATGM fire, killing seven and wounding 19.On 10 August, Northern Command ordered the division to take key terrain in and around Rashaf by 11 August, a mission accomplished on 12 August. However, it did not complete the mission of opening a logistic route in the vicinity of the Hubkan Junction. The final major operation of the division was a heli-landing operation near Yatar village. After dropping the paratroopers at the landing site, an IAF CH-53 heavy-lift transport helicopter was shot down, and all five crew were killed. The paratroopers were preparing to continue their attack when they were ordered to cease operations.

366 Division. Its mission was to take the Marj Ayoun area. On 9 August, its preliminary attack was stopped by Hezbollah. On 11–12 August, the division could not effectively resume its attacks and did not accomplish its missions.

Map 8 presents the final IDF ground positions and provides an assessment of the state of Hezbollah rocket-launching sites at the time when the ceasefire agreement ending the war went in to effect.

As the Litani Offensive pushed northwards through destroyed towns, olive groves, and tobacco fields, the Israelis confronted stiff resistance and difficult terrain. Many of the roads that led north had been cratered by air and artillery strikes and were littered with wrecked vehicles. Amid the fighting, IDF units continued having trouble in coordinating their assaults and countering Hezbollah ATGMs. This was especially prevalent among reservists, who demonstrated poor proficiency in combined arms tactics. Logistical problems also hampered progress, as the IDF had difficulties supplying food and water to sustain their soldiers inside Lebanon, forcing many to forage supplies from civilians.

The inability of the Israelis to take southern Lebanon rapidly, as they had done in the 1980s, further solidified the will of Hezbollah and its supporters to resist. Hezbollah resistance made it impossible for the Israelis to reach the Litani River. In the past, Israel could occupy the whole South

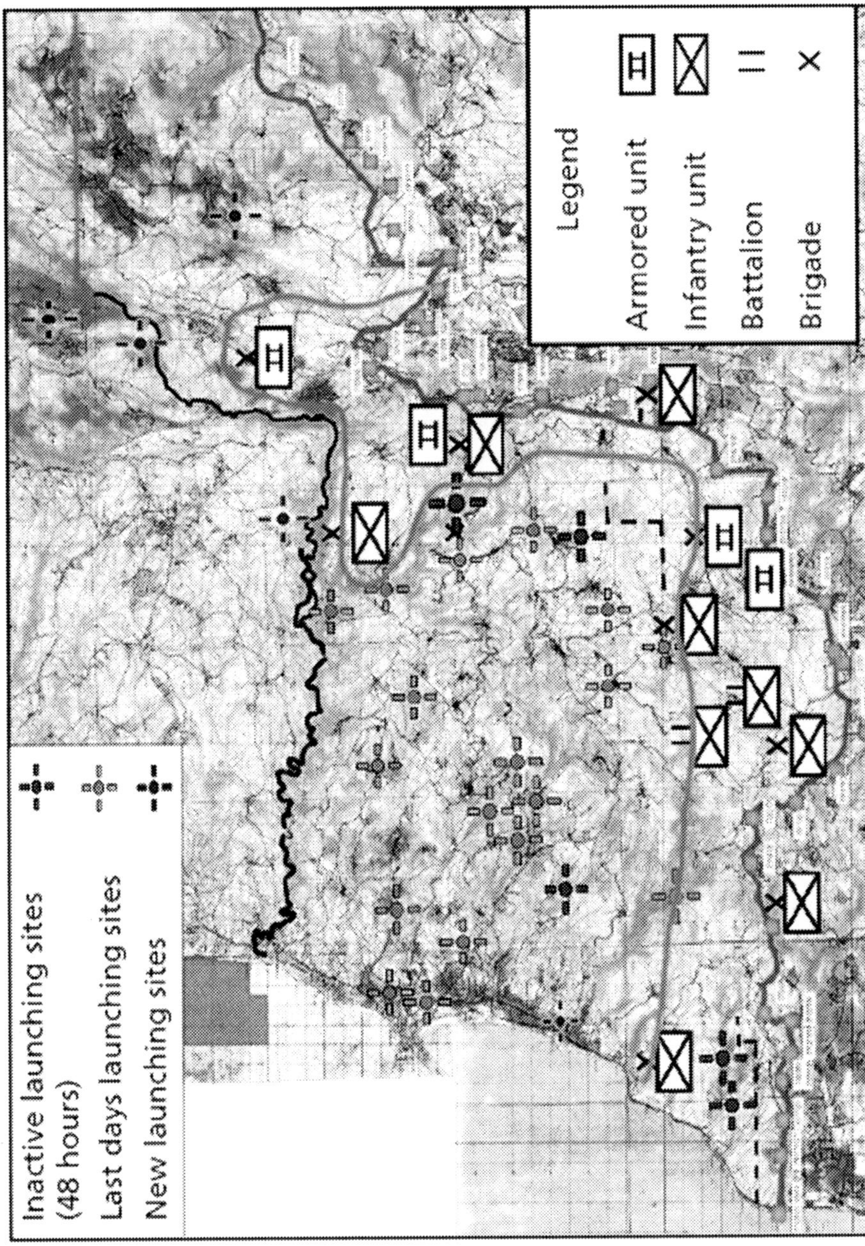

Map 8: Final IDF Positions

in five or six days. Now, after twenty-three days of fighting they found it difficult to take a single village.

Hezbollah countered the Litani offensive by increasing the intensity of its rocket barrages, firing an estimated 250 rockets into Israel in one day. Even with 30,000 IDF soldiers operating across southern Lebanon, Hezbollah remained intact and continued attacking northern Israel. To avoid detection, fighters moved in small groups at night on all-terrain vehicles and dirt bikes, often dressed as civilians. The air campaign, while expansive, failed to destroy enough rocket systems to blunt the barrages. Ground troops could not accomplish the mission either. Hezbollah was too entrenched in southern Lebanon and the offensive was unable to dislodge them without a protracted ground war. Israel did not have the political willpower to sustain an operation of this scale and duration. Public support for the war was already plummeting within Israel and international pressure continued to mount until, on the morning of 14 August, the UN brokered ceasefire came into effect. The war was over.

While Hezbollah's television station *al-Manar* (which the IAF failed to knock off the air) continued to broadcast glowing reports of its successful battle with the IDF, Israeli state-owned television denounced the IDF and what it called idiotic military manoeuvres. Israeli print media also harassed the IDF with three front page columns asking "Was there a proper decision process? No Goals attained," and "Has the army failed?" To make matters worse, international opinion (which early on had denounced Hezbollah for the kidnapping) turned against Israel as the IAF continued to attack Lebanon's infrastructure and inadvertently kill Lebanese civilians. Like the air and ground campaign, the IDF's media campaign was floundering. Contrary to the plan, it was projecting "*a cognitive perception of defeat*" onto the IDF and the Israeli public.

Halutz, however, remained convinced that his method was still viable. Irritated by the lack of success, he replaced northern sector Commander Lieutenant General Udi Adams with his own personal representative, Major General Moshe Kaplinsky to manage the war.

The Reserves

The true magnitude of the Israeli ground forces' fragility became increasingly evident as IDF reserve units began to assemble near the border. They were poorly organised and disciplined. IDF commanders were also disturbed by their performance, noting a signal lack of discipline even among its best-trained soldiers and hesitated to put them into battle.

In the past six years, most reservists had only had a week's training. They were not properly trained for their mission. Having been engaged in policing missions in the West Bank, establishing checkpoints, hunting stone-throwing Palestinian children, they were not ready to confront real fighters like Hezbollah. A reserve engineering officer who was ordered to clear a road running into Bint Jbeil refused, his men complaining that 10 soldiers had already died there. The brigade commander had the entire platoon arrested. It was later revealed that in many cases, the reluctance to send Israeli reservists into battle against Hezbollah grew out of the realisation by commanding officers that the soldiers would have been going on suicide missions.

Many of the reserve soldiers who arrived at their bases to receive their military equipment found basic items missing from their kitbags. There was also a lack of bulletproof vests, medical vests, radios, ammunition, thermal night-vision devices, as well as food and water. Some IDF reserve units conducting cross-border attacks found themselves without basic sustenance as their supply trucks were not allowed to go forward for fear of Hezbollah's antitank missiles. In the Alexandroni Brigade, one of the unit's missions was delayed because of the lack of food and water.

Incredibly, even the reserve division commanders lacked training and were both tactically and technically deficient. Brigadier General Erez Zuckerman, who commanded the reserve armoured division, had spent most of his career as a marine commando and had never received training in the use of tanks or mechanised forces. Brigadier General Eyal Eizenberg, the commander of the reserve paratrooper division, was singled out for harsh criticism for his apparent lack of tactical proficiency. There can be little doubt that the IDF reserve forces lacked leadership, training, and equipment. This was a serious detriment as these citizen soldiers comprised nearly 80 percent of the IDF's ground forces.

Hezbollah Performance

It is also important to analyse Hezbollah's proficiency in executing its defensive operations. Guerrillas can essentially get by with simple, unsophisticated hit-and-run methods that can be executed with minimal training. Competent conventional warfare at the theatre level demands intensive training, especially for the coordination and synchronisation of large-scale manoeuvre. Hezbollah showed that non-state actors can wage conventional warfare.

Hezbollah's proficiency in 2006 was uneven. Some aspects were done very well. Its defences were systematically organised and very effective. IDF attackers were rarely able to identify Hezbollah combat positions prior to drawing fire from them, even from very short ranges. In Dayr Siryan, Israeli infantry approached to within 50-100 metres of Hezbollah fighters without spotting them; in Aytarun, tanks passed directly beneath the windows used to fire upon them, without seeing the defenders first; in Bint Jubayl, defensive positions in buildings were still invisible to infantry advancing up directly adjoining streets; in At Tayyibah, Hezbollah defenders opened fire undetected from a range of 50 metres. Movement by alternate and supplementary positions within buildings often enabled urban defenders to remain concealed even after extended firing; especially in villages near the Israeli border, tunnels were dug between buildings to facilitate concealed movement. In the border area, combat preparations initiated years before the war resulted in civilian homes whose construction was influenced by military tactical considerations: buildings in key locations were discovered with thick, reinforced walls on the sides facing likely approach routes from Israel. Other indoor combat positions near the border had sandbags or other reinforcements hidden in the interior to strengthen walls facing intended engagement areas. Outdoor and rural positions were sometimes very elaborately prepared, with concrete dugouts, multiple chambers, concealed entry and exit points, and carefully camouflaged firing positions. Antitank missile positions were especially difficult to locate, given the extended range of ATGM engagements and Hezbollah's success at concealing launchers and crews.

Defences for rural *Katyusha* rocket launch areas were especially intricate, well-camouflaged, and carefully prepared—sometimes including hydraulically raised and lowered launch tubes, concrete-reinforced caches, showers for troops, multiple entrances and exits, and interconnected outworks to enable concealed movement within the system.

Hezbollah fire discipline was effective and consistent. Engagements were typically initiated by coordinated, concentrated fire from multiple locations. Defenders routinely allowed lead echelons to pass, opening fire on follow-on elements once they had advanced into kill zones; locations were rarely given away by premature firing from nervous individuals.

Hezbollah effectively coordinated direct fire in support of its counterattacks, often from multiple directions. Barriers and ATGM positions were integrated with considerable skill over multi-kilometre distances: east of Ghanduriyih, for example, a series of minefields were laid in locations that canalised Israeli columns into engagement areas exposed to ATGM fire from concealed launchers located north of the Litani River some five kilometres away. Hezbollah mortar fire was also consistently accurate and responsive.

On the minus side, Hezbollah demonstrated no ability to control or coordinate the manoeuvre of large formations. Counterattacks, for example, never exceeded platoon strength, and many were considerably smaller, with 3-5 soldiers; small detachments often fought isolated actions; and while perhaps 60-100 commandos were moved over great distances, no large reserve was held or manoeuvred against IDF movements. Movements of Hezbollah forces within their forward defences were small-scale and over short distances. This should be seen in context: the entire size of the Hezbollah combatant force in southern Lebanon was probably well under 7,000, hence battalion- or brigade-size manoeuvre would be unrealistic.

Hezbollah demonstrated only limited combined-arms cooperation. They frequently used ATGMs in concert with small arms and heavy machine guns in direct fire, and they made significant use of mortars—but rarely were direct and indirect fires combined against single targets or in single engagement areas. There were exceptions: at Bint Jubayl, for example, a Hezbollah counterattack combined direct fire support with suppressive indirect fire from remotely located mortars, which continued as Hezbollah ground forces advanced; at At Tayyibah on 28-29 July, IDF units simultaneously received ATGM and mortar fire, each from ranges of several kilometres; at Ghanduriyih, IDF attackers similarly received simultaneous ATGM and mortar fire; the Israeli advance through the Saluqi valley had to clear minefields under ATGM fire. Such exceptions were uncommon, however. Hezbollah showed no ability to coordinate mines, obstacles, direct and indirect fire in a single, synchronised defence, or to do so over any extended front.

Few Hezbollah units showed ability to react to changing conditions. Counter-attackers were taken under surprise fire from previously concealed IDF positions away from the assault objective, for example, often halted and fell back in disorder rather than reorienting to the new threat, redirecting suppressive fire, and continuing the advance. Where Hezbollah organised linear defences, these were often outflanked by Israeli attackers; the defenders, typically either fought on in the same positions or simply withdrew, rather than forming a new front to meet the assault. Although Hezbollah made apparent attempts to monitor Israeli communications networks, some of which (such as medical evacuation nets) operated in the clear, there is no evidence they were able to exploit any information gained.

Hezbollah direct fire marksmanship was very uneven. Small arms fire, for example, was systematically inaccurate and caused few casualties. Hezbollah ATGM crews, by contrast, could strike targets from extraordinary ranges: Israeli armoured vehicles were regularly hit by missiles fired from 4-5 kilometres away. Hezbollah frequently fired such missiles in salvos at single targets, however, and IDF armoured vehicles normally manoeuvred evasively and used smoke for obscuration, once under attack. The result of this combination was that the ratio of ATGM hits to total launches was very low. In the Saluqi valley fighting, missiles were fired in volleys of perhaps a dozen rounds at a time, of which 1-2 would hit their targets; an IDF combat engineer battalion in Ghanduriyih received 6-8 ATGM launches while manoeuvring at night with no hits; on the night of 12 August, a formation of more than 15 tanks received over a dozen *Kornets* fired from the village of Yuhmur, north of the Litani River roughly five kilometres away, suffering three hits, all of them against stationary vehicles—no moving targets were hit; in another engagement at At Tayyibah, one of a volley of four *Saggers* hit an IDF D9 armoured bulldozer; the survivors used smoke, but Hezbollah continued firing without further success. The net result was a potentially lethal threat, but a very large expenditure of missiles per target struck.

The Israelis realised, in retrospect, that Hezbollah constituted a different type of enemy than the IDF had confronted in the West Bank or in Gaza. This led to an understanding of the need to prepare in the future for a different kind of war, a limited war of a state against a non-state actor operating from the territory of a failed state that does not control its own territory. Hezbollah fought as a guerrilla force, though in some areas it possessed state-like capabilities, acquired from supporting states. It used various kinds of guided missiles: anti-tank, anti-aircraft, and land-to-sea missiles as well as assault UAVs, and had the ability to strike deep in Israel's home front.

Hezbollah was an adversary that was neither the low-end nor the high-end threat that Israel had envisioned in its operational concept. It was trained and organised into small units and armed with effective standoff weapons, including ATGMs, RPGs (including highly effective RPG-29s), rockets, mortars, mines, IEDs, UAVs, and MANPADS. Hezbollah also occupied prepared defensive positions in Lebanon's difficult hilly terrain and urban areas. Overall, this kind of adversary presented a qualitative problem that required joint, combined-arms fire and manoeuvre. In the aftermath of the Second Lebanon War, this is the enemy that the IDF set about preparing to fight.

Hezbollah also had a decentralised command and control in tactical operations. In the Israeli case, involvement of the General Staff was too deep and even unnecessary. It inhibited the Regional Command in discharging its duty and led to preoccupation of the General Staff with micromanaging the tactical issue at the expense of dealing with the overall strategic view of the campaign. Units continued to receive contradictory, changed orders, from their higher headquarters. Finally, the threats posed by rockets created a set of strategic issues within Israel on three levels:

(a) The fact that the IDF could not stop short-range rockets created a sense of vulnerability in the Israeli population.

(b) The prospect of long-range rockets with larger payloads, particularly if their accuracy is improved, will eventually put all of Israel at risk of attack. Hezbollah's challenge will be finding ways to hide these more-capable systems so that interdicting them, as occurred during the war in 2006, becomes impossible.

(c) Hezbollah's rockets also put IAF air bases at risk.

Losing Support for the War

The important issue in assessing the Second Lebanon War is not determining who won and who lost. Secretary-General Nasrallah vastly underestimated the Israeli response to the abductions of the IDF soldiers. Air strikes and infantry sweeps probably eliminated about half of the longer-range rockets that were not expended, as well as a large number of launchers. Hezbollah's elaborate infrastructure in south Lebanon was disrupted, and many of its facilities in the Beirut suburbs were razed. By the time Hezbollah was pushing for a cease-fire, which winners do not normally do, its fighters were trapped in a box between the Israeli border, a blockaded coast, blown bridges and roads leading north, and a large IDF force in Marjayoun, poised to march up the Beka to the east. Nevertheless, the IDF, for the first time, looked incompetent.

Several incidents combined to put external and internal pressure on Israel to end operations in Lebanon. The first was on 30 July, when an IAF airstrike destroyed a building in Qana, a town located 10 kilometres south of Tyre, killing more than 20 people, many of them children. This incident drew both the ire of the international community and charges that the IDF was deliberately targeting civilians. Qana was a turning point. Prior to the airstrike, there had been some level of support for Israel among the international community, and the leaders of the Group of Eight had issued a condemnation of Hezbollah's actions on 16 July. In the aftermath of the incident, the US began pressing Israel to reach a ceasefire. On 5 August, the US and France introduced the text that would ultimately become UN Resolution 1701, which was approved unanimously by the UN Security Council on 11 August.

Two other events turned Israeli domestic opinion against the war. On 6 August, a *Katyusha* rocket launched by Hezbollah killed 12 IDF paratroopers at Kfar Giladi. The incident was broadcast on Israeli media and had an immense impact on public morale. Later that day, a Hezbollah rocket hit Haifa, killing three civilians. This was the moment when public opinion switched. Two days earlier, there was a feeling that the whole country was united. But on 6 August, a sense of distaste and disgust in Israeli domestic opinion sunk in.

The End of the War

The ceasefire agreement went into effect at 0800 hours on Monday, 14 August. Hezbollah moved its forces back from the border, and UN peacekeepers moved in behind them. 120 IDF soldiers had been killed and more than 1,000 had been wounded in the war; there were also 37 Israeli civilian deaths, mostly as a result of *Katyusha* fire. Estimates of the number of Lebanese civilians killed range from 900 to 1,100, and the reported number of Hezbollah members killed ranges from 250 to 800. Beyond these figures, however, the war was a disaster for Israel. Just by surviving and showing that it could continuously launch rockets at Israel, Hezbollah was able to claim victory. Indeed, 217 rockets fell on Israel on 13 August. The IDF's reputation as a competent military force—a reputation key to Israel's deterrent power—also suffered because of both the indecisive way in which its operations were commanded and its poor performance in the field. These shortcomings were mainly due to Israel's lack of preparation for the war in which it found itself.

COMMENTS AND OBSERVATIONS

Overview

The Second Lebanon War demonstrated that combat forces with advanced and optimal technology for facing a conventional enemy may be vulnerable to an asymmetric attack aimed at neutralising the stronger side's technological advantages while miring it in political problems that negate its military advantages. A central challenge of such a conflict is that it becomes difficult for democracies to fight and imposes various constraints, including:

(a) Ensuring efforts are made to reduce harm to civilians and avoid collateral damage.

(b) Producing convincing evidence that such efforts are, in fact, made.

(c) Producing evidence as close as possible to real time in order to refute false charges made regarding civilian casualties and disproportionate use of force.

The military strategic objectives defined for the IDF when it embarked on the Second Lebanon War comprised a number of elements some measurable and others whose success, if at all achieved, was essentially difficult to gauge. The objectives were:

(a) *Stopping terror activities against Israel from Lebanon's sovereign territory.* To considerable extent activities after the war suggest that this was achieved,

(b) *Implementing Lebanon's responsibility and its control in the south of the country.* The deployment and activity of the South Lebanon Army and deployment of UN forces have pushed Hezbollah northward, and the organisation's freedom of activity in the south has decreased significantly.

(c) *Inflicting substantial damage on Hezbollah.* The extent of damage inflicted on the organisation can be assessed in context of the organisation's standing in Beirut. The organisation sustained an unprecedented blow after it suffered about 1,500 casualties, including about 500 deaths. A considerable number of villages were abandoned or destroyed, its long-range rocket facility was almost totally destroyed, and its logistical rear in Baalbek was hit. All these indicate a very heavy toll on the organisation.

(d) *Exerting pressure to return the hostages.* Assessment of the achievement of this objective is well-nigh impossible.

The IDF's performance can be assessed on two levels: the first relates to performance vis-a-vis the degree to which the strategic objectives that the IDF set out to achieve in the war were in fact achieved; the second relates to the IDF's operational performance in the war.

The 2006 Lebanon War was costly for both, Israel and Lebanon. The Lebanese had not experienced destruction on this level since their civil war. An estimated 1,191 Lebanese civilians died and thousands more were wounded or displaced. The war also destroyed over 640 kilometres of Lebanese roads and 350 schools, while severely damaging an estimated 900 commercial structures. For Israel, the costs were lower: the rocket attacks killed 43 Israeli civilians and wounded 690 others. The war also temporarily displaced an estimated 500,000 Israelis from their homes in northern Israel. Economically, Lebanon lost an estimated $12 billon; Israel lost $4.8 billon.

119 Israeli soldiers, sailors, and airmen died in the war. Two years later, during the summer of 2008, the number rose to 121, after Hezbollah returned the bodies of SSGs Goldwasser and Regev, the two soldiers kidnapped during the 12 July 2006 raid that sparked the war. Calculating the number of Hezbollah fighters killed in the war is difficult, given the questionable reliability of Hezbollah and Israeli reporting on the figure. Most estimates put the figure around 500—a significant amount of losses for 30 days of combat.

Despite its high casualties, Hezbollah's performance in the war exceeded expectations. While fighting against a technologically superior adversary, Hezbollah maintained a strong defence that slowed and bloodied the Israeli advance. At the same time, they were able to maintain a steady stream of rocket fire into northern Israel that provoked the Israelis into retaliatory strikes that caused civilian casualties that Hezbollah exploited for political advantage. The rocket campaign also eroded Israeli support for the war by making life difficult for the citizens of northern Israel.

While Hezbollah was celebrating its military and political victory, Israel was in a state of shock. The most modern military in the Middle East, which had defeated the combined power of the Arab world on several occasions, struggled to combat a group of militants. Seeking answers, the Israeli government set-up a commission, headed by Eliyahu Winograd, a former Israeli Supreme Court Justice. The Winograd Commission concluded that in the lead-up to the war, the Prime Minister made up his mind hastily and the Chief of Staff responded to the taking of Israeli hostages impulsively. The report added that poor leadership, coupled with an unprepared military, created a flawed strategy for destroying or marginalising Hezbollah. The Commission added that the war was a missed opportunity to deal a devastating blow to an enemy of Israel. See Appendix B.

Although it failed to achieve its major objectives, Israel did achieve some valuable strategic gains. The terms of the ceasefire, as stated in UN Resolution 1701 (See Appendix C), expanded the UN presence in southern Lebanon and deployed 15,000 soldiers from the Lebanese Army to secure the border. As a result of this deployment the Israeli northern border has enjoyed a state of peace since 2006. Hezbollah, however, has not disarmed and, in fact, it restocked its arsenals with aid from Iran and Syria. The Lebanese government agreed not to search for Hezbollah weapons caches, nor confiscate their weapons, unless displayed in public. Hezbollah has also rebuilt a large portion of its infrastructure in southern Lebanon, despite the presence of UN and Lebanese observers.

Since 2006, Hezbollah has been relatively quiet, suggesting the 2006 War acted as a deterrent for future Hezbollah incursions into Israel. Nasrallah even admitted that if he had known the consequences of the 12 July raid, he would not have ordered it. Moreover, the Israeli military has used the lessons learned from this war to improve its military readiness for future wars against more sophisticated enemies. If Hezbollah and Israel go to war again, the outcome may be quite different. As Israeli Defence minister, Ehud Barak, warned, in September 2010, "Hezbollah will not surprise us again."

Israeli Air Attacks on Lebanon

There is little evidence that the IAF succeeded in wiping out the medium and long-range rocket capability of Hezbollah, in the first days of the war. Hezbollah had probably known that the Israelis were collecting information on rocket platforms and launchers and managed to move them without being detected. Most of the locations attacked by the Israeli air force were therefore empty.

Israel overstated the effectiveness of the air war against Hezbollah. It failed to hit any of the Hezbollah leaders in spite of dropping 23 tons of bombs on its alleged headquarters bunker. *Al-Manar* TV station only went dark for two minutes after a strike before it was back into the air. The TV station was bombed 15 times during the war but never faltered after the first hiccup.

During the war the Israeli Air Force flew 11,897 combat missions, which was more than the number of sorties during the 1973 October War (11,223) and almost double the number during the 1982 First Lebanon War (6,052). The Israeli artillery fired 170,000 shells, more than twice the number fired in the 1973 October War. The Israeli Navy fired 2,500 shells. The combined effect of the massive air and artillery bombardment on Hezbollah capacity to fire short-range *Katyusha* rockets on northern Israel was very meagre. According to the findings of the post-war military investigations the IDF shelling succeeded only in destroying about 100 out of 12,000 *Katyusha* launchers. The massive fire led to a severe shortage of ammunition towards the end of the war.

The IDF had prepared a list before the war on potential Hezbollah targets, identified by the Israeli intelligence, to be struck in case of renewed hostilities. By the fourth day of the war the IDF ran out of targets, as all the 83 targets on the list had already been hit. Large parts of the Lebanese civilian infrastructure were destroyed, including 640 kilometres of roads, 73 bridges, and 31 other targets such as Beirut's Rafiq Hariri International Airport, ports, water and sewage treatment plants, electrical facilities, 25 fuel stations, 900 commercial structures, up to 350 schools and two hospitals, and 15,000 homes. Some 130,000 more homes were damaged.

Hezbollah Rocket Attacks on Israel

On 16 July, eight employees of the Israel Railways were killed by direct rocket hits on the Haifa train depot. Civilians in the border communities were hurt in the initial fire on IDF positions for the cross-border raid. Two Israeli civilians were killed in an attack near the air force base at Mount Meron on 14 July. Since Hezbollah rockets were not very accurate it is unclear whether civilians were intentionally targeted in these attacks. After the attack on Haifa, however, Hezbollah made no attempt to cover this fact.

Hezbollah TV station *al-Manar* warned, both in Arabic and Hebrew, specific Israeli communities about future rocket attacks. Similarly, Hezbollah sent text messages to warn Israeli residents to evacuate their homes to avoid being targeted by rocket attacks. During the war, the Hezbollah rocket force fired between 3,970 and 4,228 rockets at a rate of more than 100 per day, unprecedented since the Iran–Iraq War. About 95% of these were 122 mm *Katyusha* rockets, which carried warheads up to 30 kilograms and had a range of up to 30 kilometres. An estimated 23% of these rockets hit cities and built-up areas across northern Israel. One million Israelis had to stay near or in bomb shelters or security rooms, with some 250,000 civilians evacuating the north and relocating to other areas of the country.

After the high number of Lebanese civilian casualties in the Qana airstrike, on 30 July, Israel announced a unilateral freeze in its air attacks on Lebanon. Hezbollah then halted its own rocket attacks on Israel. When Israel resumed its air attacks on Lebanon, Hezbollah followed suit and recommenced rocket attacks on Israeli targets. Hezbollah rocket attacks also targeted and succeeded in hitting military targets in Israel. The Israeli military censorship was very strict and explicitly forbade Israel-based media from reporting such incidents. A notable exception was the rocket attack of 6 August, on a company of IDF reservists assembling in the border community of Kfar Giladi, which killed 12 soldiers and wounded several others. Initially, Israel did not confirm that the victims were military.

Short-range rockets are hard to find from the air for four principal reasons:

(a) They are relatively small and, compared with intermediate- and long-range rockets, are easier to hide.

(b) Smaller rockets do not need to be attended by crews, and they can be fired remotely or with timers.

(c) Unlike larger rockets, short-range rockets do not need to be mounted on vehicles, do not create a significant back blast, and do not have to be moved into an open area and prepared for launch by a crew before being fired.

(d) Compared with larger rockets, whose physical size when on the launcher and whose launch blast make them easier to find and attack, smaller rockets have a smaller signature.

The most important observation to be made about the Second Lebanon War is that the IDF's operational concept did not present a vision for the military to achieve the objectives set by the politicians. The concept, which was based largely on standoff fires, did not force Hezbollah to meet Israeli demands. Standoff fires were unable to significantly reduce Hezbollah's ability to continue firing short-range rockets against the Israeli homeland. When standoff fires did not resolve the conflict, the Israeli General Staff had no plan to fall back on. The absence of plans not only severely encumbered the IDF ability to advance quickly and on the basis of a common language for operations that were drilled according to the plans while adjusting them to the circumstances, but it also limited the effective readiness on other levels as well. The ground war thus became an act of improvisation by the Israeli Army, which was not trained or prepared for the war it found itself in.

The Ground War

Hezbollah engaged in guerrilla warfare with IDF ground forces, fighting from well-fortified positions, often in urban areas, and attacking with small, well-armed units. Hezbollah fighters were highly trained, and equipped with flak jackets, night-vision goggles, communications equipment, and sometimes with Israeli uniforms. During engagements with the IDF, Hezbollah concentrated on inflicting losses on the IDF, believing an unwillingness to absorb steady losses to be Israel's strategic weakness.

Hezbollah countered IDF armour through the use of sophisticated Russian-made anti-tank guided missiles (ATGMs). 52 *Merkava* main battle tanks were damaged (45 of them by different kinds of ATGM), missiles penetrated 22 tanks, but only 5 tanks were destroyed, one of them by an IED. Hezbollah caused additional casualties with ATGMs to collapse buildings onto Israeli troops sheltering inside. As a result, IDF units did not linger in any one area for an extended period of time. Hezbollah fighters often used tunnels to emerge quickly, fire an anti-tank missile, and then disappear again.

On 14 July 2006, INS Hanit a *Sa'ar* 5-class corvette of the Israeli Navy, suffered damage after being struck by a Hezbollah anti-ship missile. Four crew members were killed during the attack but INS Hanit stayed afloat, extricated itself and made the journey back to Ashdod port for repairs on its own power.

The Gaps between Strategic Objectives and Execution

The confrontation between the State of Israel and a sub-state entity such as Hezbollah reflects a fundamental asymmetry: a terrorist organisation, free of state responsibility, hides within the civilian population and uses it as human shields and even cannon-fodder for propaganda purposes—and then directs its activity to attack Israeli civilians. Another dimension of the asymmetry is the war's objectives: for Hezbollah, the fact that it did not surrender to Israel was seen as a victory, while for Israel an end state in which it had not decisively bested a terrorist organisation was seen as a defeat.

In the absence of a clear victory for Israel, the fuzzy picture of the war's outcomes that Hezbollah presented to the Lebanese public allowed the organisation and its leader to declare "a divine victory," whereas the Israeli side was shrouded in internal criticism, committees, and commissions of inquiry on the subject of the failure. Only much later did Hezbollah admit to the mistakes it had made and the price it paid (the project to reconstruct the ruins concluded only seven years later), and in practice has avoided resuming proactive attacks on Israel from the Lebanese border (in part because of the circumstances that developed in Syria).

Israel's failures in its prosecution of the war can be summarised as follows:

(a) There was no understanding that the quick Israeli response in heavily damaging Hezbollah's strategic capabilities would lead to a war, and no state of war was ever declared. Avoiding the designation of a military operation as "war" also stemmed from psychological blocks and political barriers. For this reason, many political and military systems, including the civilian front, did not shift into emergency mode. The decision to call up the reserves came late, and once it came, progressed slowly. Moreover, the forces called up were not appropriately prepared before the ground offensive, despite the fact that it started only about a month after the war broke out. Also, there was little willingness to take risks in the use of force, as required in a state of war.

(b) The IDF, which for several years had concentrated on the ongoing conflict in the Palestinian arena, had reduced readiness in the northern sector and had not prepared for a high intensity confrontation with Hezbollah. It assumed—erroneously—that the operational experience it had accrued in fighting Palestinian terrorism had trained it sufficiently to face Hezbollah. The damage to IDF readiness was evident in the state of the emergency depots of the reserve divisions and in the command and control capabilities of the division command centres, which had lost their combat competency.

(c) The IDF did not have an appropriate response to the continued short-range rocket launches and to Hezbollah's underground infrastructures where the launchers were concealed and protected, so that even the paralysing of Hezbollah's strategic launch systems and destroying 90 percent of the mid-range rocket launchers was nullified because of the inability to suppress the short-range rocket launchers.

(d) On the eve of the war, the General Staff approved an updated IDF concept and mode of operations, but the army still had many reservations and therefore it was not assimilated within the forces on the ground. Consequently, there was confusion at the General Staff level and among the field commanders regarding the doctrine on the deployment of forces.

(e) An asymmetrical confrontation is manifested not only in the deployment of force but also in a war's objectives. Hezbollah considered survival as victory. By contrast, Israel's political goals required it to achieve a situation on the ground that the enemy would not be able to manipulate to its own advantage. It had to significantly reduce Hezbollah's ability to damage Israel's civilian and strategic rear.

(f) In a political campaign, it is impossible to attain meaningful results without clear successes on the battlefield. In Israel, for a political campaign to succeed, five factors are relevant:

   (i) International legitimacy, i.e., Israel is not blamed for starting the war.

(ii) Clear success on the battlefield that translates into Israel's ability to force its ceasefire conditions on the enemy.

(iii) Full use of the regional and international environment to promote Israel's political goals.

(iv) Coordination with the US on war goals and the ways to attain them, including consideration of US interests.

(v) Avoid war crimes while reducing collateral damage and, to the extent possible, prevention of harm to non-combatants on the enemy's side.

Unmanned Aerial Vehicles in Asymmetric Warfare

The 2006 Second Lebanon War represents a turning point in the use of Unmanned Aerial Vehicles (UAVs). This was the first war in history that recorded more unmanned flight hours than manned fighter aircraft flight hours, featuring sustained UAV use without breaks in situational awareness. The overall number of Israel's UAV flight hours during the Second Lebanon War was approximately 16,000. On average, there were some 21 UAVs in the air at any given time. The war marked a new role for the UAV in asymmetric warfare, yet as in other technological fields, the margin of asymmetry between the sides was maintained.

During the war the IDF employed a number of UAV models, including the Hermes 450 and Searcher. These UAVs were operated by the IAF as part of their aerial forces, while the Israeli ground forces used tactical drones. The UAVs played a major role in several of the conflict's important aerial missions, including the Launcher Hunt mission, which involved a capability developed by the IAF for destroying from the air mobile targets that can change location with short time frames. This mission included UAVs continuously patrolling the airspace above ground-to- ground missile and rocket launching areas in Lebanon, and made use of diverse types of sensors to discover missile launchers before or after launch and enable their destruction by precision weaponry. This method of operation led to the destruction of more than ninety mobile launchers and another thirty launch tubes during the war.

Hezbollah also employed UAVs in this conflict; these were shot down by Israeli fighter jets. According to declassified data, Hezbollah launched four UAVs toward Israel, apparently Iranian models designed for both intelligence gathering and attack that were refitted to meet Hezbollah needs.

According to reports, these UAVs were loaded with explosives, and the timing of their launch indicates night operation capabilities. To deal with this new threat, the IAF had to make adjustments to its radar capabilities to enable them to identify relatively small aircraft flying slowly at low altitudes.

Extensive use of UAVs, inter alia, enables achievement of military and political goals within generally imposed constraints: UAVs have capabilities that allow for increased situational awareness, which aids in improved intelligence; improves the ability to distinguish between combatants and non-combatants; enhances capabilities for precise attacks, thus reducing collateral damage; and provides greater ability to broadcast up-to-date information in real time, including for public relations and media purposes. Overall, UAVs assist in maintaining legitimacy for the state to continue acting against the enemy. In addition, they help reduce physical risk to the party operating them, and help overcome some of the barriers facing operators of manned combat vehicles. UAVs will be one of the prominent weapons assisting military powers in coping with the asymmetric challenge.

The Use of Helicopters

Compared to combat against regular forces, achieving victory in warfare against non-state actors is much more complex because it cannot be attained by a one-time action. While military activity should not be over-emphasised, it remains a critical component of warfare. The military modus operandi is to eliminate belligerent non-state actors through exhaustion, attrition, and weakening of guerrilla forces, with the main objective being to prevent losses and minimise attrition on their side. Furthermore, the regular army must bring its technological superiority to bear on the fighting. From the military aspect, the attack helicopter is the ideal platform for fighting guerrillas.

Attack helicopters have several prominent advantages. First, their mobility is not affected by terrain, and they have the capacity to operate at longer ranges compared to ground forces. The second advantage is the ability to deploy force at short notice. An attack helicopter task force can be placed in relatively well-protected bases, unlike ground-based task forces. In many battles against guerrilla forces, the conquest of territory is pointless.

Another advantage inherent in attack helicopters is the range of precision weapons they can carry as well as their firepower at extended ranges, i.e., mobility combined with firepower. Attack helicopters can accompany helicopters ferrying ground-based task forces to special operations while providing proximate air support and cover for landing and evacuation from the area of action. The final advantage is the attack helicopters' versatility. Guerrilla warfare is characterised by non-frontal fighting, and guerrilla forces can attack anywhere at any time. It is impossible to maintain masses of ground forces everywhere at all times, because it is very difficult to predict where and when the guerrilla forces might attack. By contrast, attack helicopters can quickly reach any area of activity and provide the required firepower.

At the same time, helicopters have several drawbacks. The main disadvantage lies in the fact that this very sophisticated and expensive platform is vulnerable to attack by simple, cheap arms. A helicopter flying at low height is exposed to anti-aircraft fire, such as cannons, machine guns, and shoulder-held rocket launchers. Another drawback is the difficulty of operating attack helicopters in difficult weather conditions. Visibility (night time, fog, etc.) limits their use as well, though this factor is gradually being mitigated by advanced night vision systems.

Despite their vulnerability, the nature of a helicopter's warfare system allows it to launch guided missiles from long distances, thereby surprising guerrilla forces. By the time they manage to regroup, the helicopter can be long gone from the fire zone. The *Apache's* "fire-and-forget" ability is an excellent example of a regular army's ability to use its technological superiority against guerrilla forces. The combination of great mobility, short response times and the concentration of heavy firepower makes attack helicopters an effective, lethal weapon system in confronting guerrilla forces and/or terrorists. In addition, the helicopters' effectiveness comes to the fore due to the fact numerous confrontations in the last few decades have taken place in densely populated urban settings, requiring the ability to cause pinpoint damage so as to minimise casualties among non-combatant civilians. Attack helicopters as a weapons system thus incorporate technologies supporting operational needs as well as the desire to reduce the number of casualties to the civilian population.

The importance of the attack helicopter was discovered during the prolonged war against Hezbollah. The IDF incorporated the airborne element in southern Lebanon, with one of the main tools being the attack helicopter. There is no doubt that the use of attack helicopters highlighted the IDF's military and technological might in the anti-terror campaign. In addition, attack helicopters, when used to provide proximate aerial support, reduced the number of infantry casualties.

The scope of missions carried out by attack helicopters in Lebanon were a manifestation of their inherent operational capabilities. In Lebanon, the IDF encountered two major problems: the first, infantry and armoured units were caught in Hezbollah ambushes; the second was the IDF's attempt to identify and destroy the *Katyusha* launchers that were shelling northern Israel, a difficult and frustrating task. The attempt to identify the launchers required real-time intelligence, attained by UAVs and other intelligence tools. The moment a *Katyusha* launcher was identified attack helicopters (or the artillery) were called in to strike at the launcher and its operators. Sometimes the launcher would be identified only after rockets had already been fired, at which point the objective was to disarm and prevent further use.

The Media as a Weapon in Asymmetrical Conflict

This was not the traditional war between Israel and an Arab state but an asymmetrical war, between a state (Israel) and a militant, secretive, religiously fundamentalist sect or faction, Hezbollah, the Party of God, often referred to as a state within a state.

It is important to assess the power of communication networks, such as the newspapers published and distributed throughout the Arab world, and even more crucial, the two cable television networks: *Al-Jazeera,* the most popular TV network in the region broadcasting out of Qatar, and *Al-Arabiya*, the second most popular network, broadcasting out of nearby Dubai. *Al-Jazeera* brilliantly reflects and feeds the mood of the Arab streets, which is hostile to the West and Israel, while *Al-Arabiya*, financed by Saudi and Lebanese businessmen, advances a similar but more cautious agenda. In their coverage, both exploit the most sophisticated technology to carry their reports across the Middle East.

Also in this transnational world of media interconnectivity, is the Internet. During the war in Lebanon, it helped produce the first really "live" war in history. Networks actually projected in real time the grim reality of the battlefield—pictures of advancing or retreating Israeli troops in southern Lebanon, homes and villages being destroyed during bombing runs, old people wandering aimlessly through the debris, some tailed by children hugging tattered dolls, Israeli airplanes attacking Beirut airport,

Hezbollah rockets striking northern Israel and Haifa, forcing thousands to evacuate their homes and move into underground shelters—all conveyed live, as though the world had a front-row seat on the blood and gore of modern warfare.

Journalists employed both the camera and the computer, and, with the help of portable satellite dishes and video phones, streamed or broadcast their reports from hotel roofs and hilltops, as they covered the movement of troops and the rocketing of villages—often, revealing sensitive information to the enemy. The camera and the computer have become weapons of war. Technology enables journalists to be a powerful influence on public opinion and governmental attitudes and actions; it also became an extremely valuable intelligence asset for both Israel and Hezbollah, and Hezbollah especially exploited it.

Importantly, a closed society can control the image and message that it wishes to convey to the rest of the world far more effectively than an open society. During the war, no Hezbollah secrets were disclosed, but in Israel secrets were leaked, rumours spread like wildfire, leaders felt obliged to issue hortatory appeals often based on incomplete knowledge, and journalists were driven by the fire of competition to publish and broadcast unsubstantiated information. A closed society conveys the impression of order and discipline; an open society, facing reality and rumour, criticism and revelation, conveys the impression of disorder, chaos and uncertainty, but this impression can be misleading.

Hezbollah projected a very special narrative for the world that depicted a selfless movement touched by God and blessed by a religious fervour and determination to resist the enemy, the infidel, and ultimately achieve a "divine victory," no matter the cost. The narrative contained no mention of Hezbollah's dependence upon Iran and Syria for a steady flow of arms and financial resources.

A key consequence of this is that the role of the journalist has been dramatically transformed—from a quest for objectivity and fairness to an acceptance of advocacy as a tool of the craft. The journalist is increasingly acceptable as an activist player and a fiery advocate. 24/7 cable news has placed a premium on provocative chatter, not on substantive discourse. This is both noteworthy and disturbing.

Israel defended its military operations by citing two relevant articles in international law: using civilians for military cover was a war crime, and any target with soldiers hiding among civilians was considered a legitimate military target. Israel's defence, however, fell on deaf ears as daily evidence mounted of civilian deaths. Hezbollah, whenever possible, pointed reporters to civilian deaths among Lebanese, with heavy propaganda implications. Early in the war, reporters routinely stated that Hezbollah had started the war, and its casualties were a logical consequence of war. But after the first week such references were either dropped or downplayed, leaving the widespread impression that Israel was irresponsible in its prosecution of the war. Disproportionality became the war's mantra; even if Israel did not start the war, and only responded to Hezbollah's raid with a disproportionate display of military strength, wrecking Lebanon's economy, destroying its infrastructure, inflaming political passions and killing civilians with reckless abandon. "And for what?" Lebanese asked. "For eight soldiers?" Rarely in the coverage was there proportionate mention of Israeli civilian deaths suffered during Hezbollah's sustained rocket attacks.

A graphic example of disproportionality appeared on television screens on 30 July, when the Israelis bombed the Shiite village of Qana in southern Lebanon, and, according to early reports, killed 54 Lebanese civilians, mostly women and children. Most reporters described the scene as a massacre. The Israelis apologised for the loss of life and explained that they were firing at a rocket site next to the building. The location of the rocket site was considered irrelevant and earned Israel international condemnation.

Asharq Al-Awsat, one of the two Arabic-language newspapers published in London and then distributed throughout the Middle East ran 24 photographs related to the war on the front page, from 13 July to 16 August; all but two of them showed the death and destruction in Lebanon caused by Israeli attacks. Readers of the paper could have drawn only one conclusion—that Israel had made Lebanon into a killing field. Only once, on 31 July, did *Asharq Al-Awsat* show a photograph of the destruction that Hezbollah rockets were causing in Israel. This imbalance could hardly be described by as objective journalism, but it could be explained in the context of Middle East journalism, where many Arab reporters feel a nationalistic, religious or cultural prejudice against Israel. *Asharq Al-Awsat* was selling papers.

In comparison, the *BBC* had a somewhat more balanced approach. However, American Fox cable news favoured Israel, *CNN* tried to be balanced, and the three major evening news programmes on *ABC*, *CBS* and *NBC* were more critical of Israel than of Hezbollah. As in other Arab-Israeli conflicts, the Arabs were portrayed as the victims. In the war of information, news and propaganda, the battlefield central to Hezbollah's strategy, Israel lost this war.

In the middle of conflict, a single reporter with a laptop and small camera can shoot, edit, feed and do live interviews. It raises questions as to what can political leaders and military commanders do in the face of such communications technology? What effect does it have on public opinion? Does live reporting from the battlefield engender a sense of responsibility and caution? The world is in a new phase that affects the very nature of journalism and war. The challenge is much more daunting: the coverage of asymmetrical wars between states and radical, religious, ideological groups, is creating political, diplomatic, journalistic and military dilemmas few fully grasp or understand.

Civil-Military Issues, Unclear Objectives, and a Lack of Jointness

Israel experienced problems in civil-military interaction and decision-making. Discussions between senior Israeli leaders never resulted in the development of a strategy, rooted in political objectives, that could be translated into obtainable and understandable operational and tactical missions. The civilian decision-makers' lack of military experience may be partly to blame, but the situation is no different in many other countries. The viability of Israel's air-centric military strategy to coerce the Lebanese government into acting to control Hezbollah, was highly questionable.

Another factor in Israel's poor performance in Lebanon was the lack of coherence within the IDF itself when it came to issuing clear military orders that framed mission-oriented objectives. Much of the problem within the Israeli military can be traced to the new and evolving operational concept. One of the characteristics of the operational concept was the fact that it was formulated on many different levels of discussion, some of them very generalised, and on key issues, such as the relationship between the use of airpower versus ground manoeuvre, it did not explicitly take a position. This presented difficulty in translating the General Staff Command's conception to combat theories and to operational concepts on the ground. Furthermore, the language used in the concept, derived from SOD, created confusion when orders were being translated into understandable military tasks.

Also, there were problems with *jointness*. Some of the issues stemmed from the operating concept was the lack of clarity on the relationship between the use of air power versus ground power as a result of the IAF and Israeli Army not having trained and planned together. This was particularly evident in IAF close air support for ground operations. The IAF's participation in the ground battle demonstrated many flaws, stemming from planning, preparedness, and training processes involving the cooperation among the IDF branches and from wide gaps in the operational concept. Flaws that surfaced at the beginning of the war were not corrected during the war. These flaws were not local and did not affect merely the IAF's operations. Their presence is particularly grave in light of the fact that the weak points in the synergy among the forces were known throughout the IDF's wars. In any operation involving the integration of forces, the responsibility for the fact that this integration is not planned, drilled, or assimilated falls on all the parties to that cooperation.

Post-Conflict Resolution of Issues

Before its withdrawal, Israel tried to obtain guarantees or understandings from Lebanon, aiming to deploy the Lebanese Armed Forces and limit Hezbollah freedom of action. However, Lebanon insisted on the complete implementation of UN Resolution 425 and an unconditional Israeli withdrawal. The Lebanese government also stated that the Israeli withdrawal itself did not signal the end of the conflict between the two states. The outstanding issues that required resolution included those Lebanese prisoners who remained in Israel, the status of Palestinian refugees in Lebanon, compensation for damages during the Israeli occupation, and withdrawal from the Shab'a Farms area on the Lebanese-Syrian border. Israel believed that its withdrawal from southern Lebanon would remove the cause for belligerence with Hezbollah, although it ignored the other unsettled issues.

Syria was a major player in Lebanese affairs. It had insisted in linking the Lebanese-Israeli track to the Syrian-Israeli track in the Middle East peace process. That necessitated the simultaneous Israeli withdrawal from Lebanese and Syrian occupied territories, and also that Israel will not come to terms with Lebanon independently from its stance vis a vis Syria. Hence, Lebanon backed by Syria, refused to send its national troops to the South, and because it did not regard the Israeli withdrawal as being complete, since it left the issues unresolved. Hezbollah has repeated many times that it is free to continue its "resistance" as long as any occupation of Lebanese territory continues.

Israel's Goals

It was clear that the disarming of Hezbollah was a consistent goal of Israel. At the outbreak of the war, its goal was redefined as the destruction of Hezbollah, the elimination of its military, missiles capabilities, and the return of the captured soldiers. Militarily, Israel aimed to destroy and disarm Hezbollah; Strategically, it was to deter other enemies (Iran, Syria, and Palestinians). Diplomatically, it desired the deployment of multinational forces. Politically, it wanted to strengthen the 14 March coalition in Lebanon to contain Hezbollah. That converged neatly with American and European interests in weakening Iranian strategic power and with Saudi Arabia's ambition to diminish Shiite influence in the region.

During the war, the Israeli objectives were not consistent and clear. Israel tried to adjust and align them with the developments of the war. In the beginning, its goals were ambitious, but when it found them hard to achieve, it evolved and moderated them. With the continuation of the campaign and Israel's inability to prevent the firing of rockets, especially the short-range ones, Israel began calling for the elimination of Hezbollah fighters who threaten its northern border, the creation of a buffer zone south of the Litani River and the deployment of Multinational or NATO forces.

At the cessation of hostilities, both sides, Israel and Hezbollah, declared victory. It was an odd war in which both sides think they're winning. It was not easy to decide who was the victor and who was the vanquished. Analysts have different views depending on their backgrounds and opinions. In fact, each side achieved some successes and had some failures.

Impact on Lebanon

Hezbollah decided to conduct its operation unilaterally, and Israel replied with a swift, incisive escalation. Lebanon and its people did not have any choice in the situation, but they paid a heavy toll. As the war took place on Lebanese terrain, it suffered economically, socially and politically. Economic losses were huge (about $7 billion), especially for a small country with a debt that exceeds $40 billion. A great deal of infrastructure has been destroyed (estimated at $3.9 billion), most of the major bridges (80 bridges), electricity installations and residential areas (15,000 homes were destroyed by Israeli bombing). Major damage was caused to the sectors of tourism, industry and services. Another problem emerged after the war—unexploded cluster bombs, forbidden under international law, dropped by Israel, which killed or wounded more than 218 people in the south since the ceasefire in August 2006.

At the social level, the massive number of displaced persons (970,000) caused numerous problems. The government's relief effort mainly involved transferring aid supplies to local civic groups for distribution to victims, but even this modest task was hampered by incompetence and corruption. Politically, the war intensified the dispute between the Lebanese political parties, over several issues such as the need for a new 'unity government', Hezbollah's disarmament and the international tribunal on Hariri's assassination. Moreover, the war proved that Lebanon could not expect political intervention by the international community. Lebanon's alliances with United States, France and Arab countries did not prevent Israel from destroying it.

At the diplomatic level, UNSCR 1701 could be considered a gain for Lebanon. It was issued under Chapter VI of the United Nations charter not VII, as Israel preferred. Under Chapter VI, the Security Council seeks "pacific settlement of disputes" by negotiation, mediation, conciliation, or arrangements (article 33). What Israel had preferred that UNIFIL do, under Chapter VII, might have been to resort to force to implement UNSCR 1701, disarm Hezbollah, and prevent it from re-armament. The Resolution was aligned with the seven-point plan proposed by Lebanese Prime Minister Saniora, and supported the Lebanese state to extend its authority over all of its territory. This, as well as the decision to deploy 15,000 Lebanese army troops supported by 15,000 UN troops, strengthened the government and showed the importance of Lebanon's stability. Moreover, Hezbollah agreed to abide by the government decisions and facilitate the mission of the Lebanese army and UNIFIL.

For the first time in decades, the Lebanese Army executed a large deployment on the southern border. Before its withdrawal in 2000, Israel had refused and prevented any such activity. Simultaneously, the Army deployed on the Lebanese-Syrian border to control it and prevent the entry of arms.

The Position of Lebanon

While the Israeli government initially held the Lebanese government responsible for the Hezbollah attacks due to Lebanon's failure to implement UNSCR 1559 and disarm Hezbollah, Lebanon disavowed the raids, stating that the government of Lebanon did not condone them, and pointing out that Israel had a long history of disregarding UN resolutions.

Israel never declared war on Lebanon, and said it only attacked Lebanese governmental institutions which it suspected of being used by Hezbollah. The Lebanese government played a role in shaping the conflict. On 14 July 2006, the office of Lebanese Prime Minister Fouad Siniora issued a statement that called on US President George W. Bush to exert all his efforts on Israel to stop its attacks in Lebanon and reach a comprehensive ceasefire. In a televised speech the next day, Siniora called for an immediate ceasefire backed by the United Nations.

A US-French draft resolution that was influenced by the Lebanese Siniora Plan and which contained provisions for Israeli withdrawal, military actions, and mutual prisoner release was rejected by the US and Israel. Many Lebanese accused the US government of stalling the ceasefire resolution and of support of Israel's attacks. In a poll conducted two weeks into the conflict, only 8 per cent of the respondents felt that the US would support Lebanon, while 87 per cent supported Hezbollah's fight against Israel. After the attack on Qana, Siniora snubbed US Secretary of State Condoleezza Rice by cancelling a meeting with her and thanked Hezbollah for its "sacrifices for the independence and sovereignty of Lebanon."

During the war, the Lebanese Armed Forces did not engage in direct hostilities, but threatened retaliation if IDF troops pushed too far northward into Lebanon. In several instances, Lebanese troops fired anti-aircraft weapons at Israeli aircraft and attempted to disrupt landing operations.

Implications of the War

Israel's inability to win the war brought about various changes, particularly at the political and military levels. The government lost much of its credibility. People called for the prime minister and the minister of defence to resign. They blamed successive governments for allowing Hezbollah to acquire more than 12,000 missiles. Many probes on the shortcomings of the war were conducted. The generals blamed the politicians for holding back the army for several days before ordering the final push. The prime minister blamed the defence minister and the army. The defence minister accused the chief of staff, Dan Halutz, who resigned later, of creating expectations that the air force alone could destroy Hezbollah. Olmert, who suffered the most rapid plummet of public approval ratings for an Israeli prime minister in decades, was seen as being unable to guarantee Israel's security.

Militarily, the war demonstrated that, in an asymmetric war, tanks, air forces or navy are not necessarily effective. High-tech systems could easily be avoided and deceived, and ground forces, especially infantry and Special Forces and highly-trained individual combatants remain essential.

Allegations, Accusations and Reports of War Crimes

Under international humanitarian law, warring parties are obliged to distinguish between combatants and civilians, ensure that attacks on legitimate military targets are proportional, and guarantee that the military advantage of such attacks outweigh the possible harm done to civilians. Violations of these laws are considered war crimes. Various groups and individuals accused both Israel and Hezbollah of violations of these laws during the conflict, and warned of possible war crimes. These allegations included intentional attacks on civilian populations or infrastructure, disproportionate or indiscriminate attacks, the use of human shields, and the use of prohibited weapons. No formal charges have been filed against either group.

Amnesty International called on both Hezbollah and Israel to end attacks on civilian areas during the conflict, and criticised attacks against civilian villages and infrastructure by Israel. They also highlighted IDF use of white phosphorus shells in Lebanon. Human Rights Watch accused both parties of failing to distinguish between civilians and combatants, violating the principle of distinction, and committing war crimes.

On its final report, issued on 30 January 2008, the Israeli government's Winograd Commission concluded that the Israel Defence Forces did not commit violations or war crimes, as alleged by the Human Rights Watch, Amnesty International, and other NGOs. The Commission claimed that the evidence shows that the Israel Defence Forces did not target civilians, in contrast to Hezbollah and to denunciations by NGOs, and explained that terms like "war crimes" are without basis. This report also acknowledged that Israel used cluster bombs illegally.

Both sides used cluster bombs during the conflict. Israel fired 4.6 million submunitions into dozens of towns and villages in southern Lebanon in 962 separate strikes, circa 90 per cent within the final 72 hours of the war, when the conflict already had been largely resolved by UN Security Council Resolution 1701. Entire towns were covered in cluster bombs. The unguided and imprecise rockets were fired from mobile rocket launching platforms. To compensate for the inaccuracy of the rockets, the areas were flooded with munitions. Israel claimed to have warned civilians prior to a strike, and that firing was limited to open areas or military targets inside urban areas. Israel used advanced cluster munitions produced by Israel Military Industries, and large numbers of older cluster bombs, some produced in the 1970s, purchased from aging American stockpiles. These were fired by multiple rocket launchers, 155mm artillery guns, and dropped by aircraft. As many as 1 million submunitions failed to explode on impact, lingering as land mines that killed or maimed almost 200 people since the war ended. As of 2011, munitions were still causing casualties and being cleared by volunteers.

Hezbollah fired 4,407 submunitions into civilian-populated areas of northern Israel in 113 separate strikes, using Chinese made Type-81 122mm rockets, and Type-90 submunitions. These attacks killed one civilian and wounded twelve.

According to Human Rights Watch, in the last 72 hours of the war, the Israeli army flooded the region with cluster bombs. Human Rights Watch "found that the IDF's use of cluster munitions was both indiscriminate and disproportionate, in violation of IHL, and in some locations possibly a war crime" because "the vast majority [were dropped] over the final three days when Israel knew a settlement was imminent." After the ceasefire, parts of southern Lebanon remained uninhabitable due to Israeli unexploded cluster bomblets.

Also phosphorus shells were used by the IDF to attack civilian areas in Lebanon. The shells were originally designed to generate a smoke screen in a battlefield situation, but white phosphor is also especially harmful to humans because its burning will continue inside the flesh. The shelling was investigated as a violation of international law.

Psychological Warfare

During the war, the IAF dropped 17,000 leaflets over Lebanon in 47 missions, and sent more than 700,000 computerised voice messages. Many of them contained caricatures of Hassan Nasrallah and Hezbollah leading Lebanon to ruin and making civilians suffer, showing them as puppets of Iran and Syria, and calling on civilians to help remove Hezbollah. Another leaflet addressing Hezbollah fighters told them that they were lied to by their leaders, that they were "sent like sheep to be butchered, lacking military training and without proper combat gear", that they could not hope to face "highly trained soldiers that fight to protect their homeland, their people, and their home", referring to them as "mercenaries" without the support of the Lebanese public, and urging them to run and save their lives. On 26 July, Israel dropped leaflets containing illustrations of nine tombstones with the name of a dead Hezbollah fighter on each one, in response to Nasrallah "deceiving" people on the amount of Hezbollah casualties. Another leaflet urged Hezbollah fighters to stop bleeding and fighting for Nasrallah, who sat safe in a bunker, to stop fighting against Lebanese national interests, and to return to their homes and families. On 11 August, Israel dropped leaflets accusing Hezbollah of hiding its "great losses", and containing the names of 90–100 Hezbollah fighters killed. Israeli technicians also hacked into *Al-Manar* and broadcast clips, criticising Nasrallah, showing the bodies of Hezbollah fighters, footage from Israeli raids and airstrikes, and captured Hezbollah equipment.

Resolution 1701: A Fragile Truce or a Path to a Diplomatic Solution

UNSCR 1701 was adopted on 11 August 2006, after long discussions and deliberations between the Security Council members, especially France and the United States, and Israel, Lebanon and Hezbollah. The approved wording was the best possible compromise. Despite the shortcomings and ambiguity that it contains, the Resolution creates both risks and opportunities.

The UN Resolution considered Hezbollah to be responsible for what happened in Lebanon without condemning the Israeli violence and excessive destruction. It did not put clear limitations on Israel. While it called for the "the immediate cessation by Hezbollah of all attacks," it called for Israel merely to cease all "offensive military operations," a deliberately vague phrase that allows Israel to justify virtually anything as a defensive military operation. The resolution requires the Lebanese government and the United Nations forces to implement the resolutions

1559 (the disarmament of the militias) and 1680 (the demarcation of the border between Syria and Lebanon), which were not implemented completely.

Hezbollah considers itself a resistance and not a militia. It has accepted the Resolution 1701, but it is not in hurry to implement it. UNIFIL is not authorised to disarm Hezbollah, since it is working under Chapter VI, its role is to assist the Lebanese government, which cannot take any decision without Hezbollah's endorsement. The arms embargo imposed by Resolution 1701 cannot be enforced without Lebanese and Syrian cooperation, which is not actually occurring.

The participation of more than 23 nations in a strong UNIFIL peacekeeping force is a broad umbrella to ensure that Lebanese territory south of the Litani River is not used for hostile activities. UNIFIL can employ forceful means to resist attempts to prevent it from discharging its duties. It can take all necessary action to prevent hostile acts of any kind in the area and to protect civilians under imminent threat. These limitations will affect both sides, it will deny Hezbollah the freedom of action and resupply, and limit Israel's conduct of hostilities against Lebanon. The Lebanese Government, including Hezbollah ministers, had unanimously adopted UNSCR 1701, consequently it has a duty to honour the agreement it signed. The same could be said about the Israeli government.

Conclusion

The implications of the war went beyond its geographic and domestic dimensions to regional and international ones. Israel has lost its ability to deter military operations in the region; probe committees were formed to investigate the shortcomings during the war, and Israelis wanted accountability for poor decision-making during the war, which resulted in resignations. At the same time, lessons were learned. Lebanon had no breathing space after the conflict for political pressures mounted from it. The aftermath of the war became a period of internal conflict and division. Thus, Lebanon has become an arena of regional and international dispute.

ASSESSMENT AND LESSONS LEARNT

Hezbollah began to establish itself as a military power in Lebanon in 1985. Hezbollah's military organisation differs from other Arab military forces. It has the structure, organisation, and capability of a regular army, the logic of a terrorist organisation, and the modus operandi of a guerrilla group. The hope that Israel's retreat from Lebanon in May 2000 would divert Hezbollah from the military course to the political sphere was not realised. Hezbollah did enter the political arena, but it also continued to strengthen itself militarily. The withdrawal of Syrian forces from Lebanon in early 2005 was a turning point for Hezbollah and the full significance of the change in the internal balance of power in Lebanon was not appreciated in Israel. Neither the significance of the absence of Syrian power as a lever for Israeli pressure on Lebanon—and when necessary on Hezbollah—nor Hezbollah's concept of its role in the new balance of power was fully comprehended.

A Test of Strategies

The strategies employed by the IDF and Hezbollah evolved over the thirty-three days of the conflict. The core of these strategies was the respective concepts that had developed over the previous six years, but these were adapted on a constant basis in response to the way that situations unfolded.

The IDF's strategy divided Lebanon into the theatres of responsibility of the Northern Command and the air force. Southern Lebanon—the region between the Litani River and the Israeli-Lebanese border—was already in the operative jurisdiction of the Northern Command before the war. As the fighting went on, the Northern Command was responsible for a smaller area. The air force bore operational responsibility for all other Lebanese territory.

Along with the geographical division was an incomplete division of tasks resulting in a lack of clarity in conducting the war effort. In the IAFs sphere of responsibility, i.e., the entire area of Lebanon except for the south, a clear attack strategy was used. The Northern Command exerted its influence in the phase directed towards pushing Hezbollah away from the area near the Israeli border. Beyond this, there were no significant plans for dealing with the *Katyusha* rockets or for any other objective.

The IDF's reluctance to conduct ground operations in southern Lebanon had a history. It reflected the belief that the threat (*Katyusha* fire against civilians) did not justify the price i.e. the lives of combat soldiers. This meant that the solution for this operational problem was to be found elsewhere. This belief greatly affected the readiness to enter a ground conflict and the manner in which IDF forces operated. It was assumed that heavy pressure and substantial achievement in the air force's theatre of responsibility would also neutralise the threat of short range missiles from southern Lebanon. The IDF's assumption that the achievements in northern Lebanon would prevent the launching of *Katyushas* from southern Lebanon proved erroneous as Hezbollah launched 100-200 *Katyushas* per day against Israeli communities.

Only late in the conflict did the IDF comprehend the significance of its failure to stop the flow of *Katyushas*. The military leadership apparently felt that it was under no time pressure. The political leadership was responsible for this feeling, although time is a factor only partially subject to Israel's influence, if at all. The feeling of time not being a factor worked against the operational requirement. Military leadership can best achieve its objectives when it has a definite, fairly rigid time framework.

The IDF also failed to comprehend the perception of the Israeli public. The IDF evaluated the *Katyusha* phenomenon according to the number of civilian casualties. Indeed, in comparison with casualties from terrorist actions, such as suicide bombings, civilian losses in the war were few. It, therefore, seemed to the decision makers that it was possible to live with the *Katyusha* fire for an extended period. At a certain point in the war, however, and at least in part as a function of the ongoing rocket fire, the public's mood changed to a feeling of uncertainty regarding the campaign. This affected the degree of public support for the government with respect to the continuation of the fighting. Towards the end of the war, the fact that the *Katyusha* fire would be the criterion for determining who won the campaign was fully understood. The expanded ground operations were designed to deal with this bombardment, but were of no avail.

Hezbollah's strategy developed in response to Israel's actions. It strove to exploit its remaining military assets in an operational situation. The results of the IAF's attacks against Hezbollah targets in the early days of the war were a great shock to the organisation's leadership. Hezbollah had no active tools (as opposed to passive tools) for dealing with the air power unleashed in most of Lebanon's territory.

Hezbollah realised that the bombardment of Israeli communities in northern Israel and Haifa by rocket fire had greater strategic value in Israel's perception. In contrast to the initial concept of Hezbollah's *Katyusha* system as random (on both time and geographic spheres) manually operated launchings, the system was organised and prepared for firing in a regular military format. Many of the launching sites were planned and calculated in advance. Some of the sites were camouflaged and concealed to varying degrees, making it possible to use the launching equipment repeatedly. Hezbollah ground forces defended the launch pads, with the use reinforced positions and bunkers prepared in advance. Hezbollah also developed a rapid response capability to IDF activity, based on eavesdropping on IDF communications. This gave them the upper hand in many of the clashes between IDF and Hezbollah ground units.

The way that the war was conducted reflected two opposing strategies. The IDF's strategy was based primarily on air superiority, while Hezbollah's strategy utilised the high degree of impregnability of its short-range rocket system. During most of the fighting, both sides refrained from any attempt to challenge the other's strategy. Having no alternative, Hezbollah refrained from defending its assets in the north, except for the defence of its senior command system and system of operational control. The IDF, on the other hand, deliberately refrained from stopping the *Katyusha* fire with ground forces, due to faulty evaluation of the operational significance of the bombardment and concern about a ground offensive. The IDF thus found itself executing a series of ground operations designed for other operational purposes rather than focussing on the *Katyusha* system. Ground warfare, when it took place, occurred to a great extent according to rules dictated by Hezbollah. This greatly reduced the IDF's relative advantage which a large and powerful army is capable of. The IDF demonstrated a low level of military capability in the ground battles—both in planning the objective and in leadership to achieve the defined objective.

The lessons that emerge are:

- The political goals of the war, and even more so the operative military goals, should be formulated in clear language not subject to different interpretations. This allows evaluating the degree to which the goals can be accomplished. The fact that wars in the Middle East are ultimately also used to advance the political goals of the international forces operating in the region should be also be taken into account in formulating political goals.
- A serious error occurred in understanding the significance of Hezbollah's *Katyusha* system, and in evaluating the way it was operated and its results. In consequence, the IDF delayed its response to the problem, enabling Hezbollah to assume the appearance of a force whose operational capabilities were preserved up until the ceasefire.
- The ground campaign revealed serious problems in the level of planning and execution by IDF ground forces. It appears that the problem was not confined to technical aspects; it concerned fundamental aspects on which an effective military force should be based. Although the war was a limited one, it exposed the fact that there are two armed forces in the IDF: the air force and the ground forces. An attempt to explain the gap between the two forces solely in budgetary terms will not help restore the ground forces to their required performance level.
- The political and strategic consequences of the continuation of fighting beyond the first week were not completely understood. Likewise, the decisive importance of an exit strategy designed to identify the point of optimal achievement was not grasped. The political leadership surrendered to a feeling that "the world is on our side," and was blind to the IDF's clumsy operational performance.

The IDF Concept of Operations

Prior to the war a new approach to the way the IDF operates was formulated. It determined the division of authority in the General Staff as well as the system of command and control by the chief of staff over the eight different commands (regional and functional). It also stipulated the responsibility for force operation and force build-up of the different organisations. The war in Lebanon brought opposing concepts to the fore:

(a) In the years prior to the development of this new concept, the approach followed was based on the operational theatre being the central element in the management of war. The underlying idea referred to two basic elements: the first is that the operational theatre incorporates *all* the fighting components of one's forces against *all* the fighting components of the enemy in the same theatre. This approach held that there is an "ideal" division into operational theatres that satisfies the above requirements.

(b) The second notion related to the *command* of the theatre. This approach determines that command of the operational theatre has to be given to the service which is the only party capable of coordinating all military activity in the theatre, and thus has the capability to formulate a systemic approach to conducting the campaign. The basic assumption of this approach is that because of this only the chief of staff is able to exercise actual command of the full operational theatre, as only he perceives the full systemic picture and thus the is capable of commanding all the IDF's operational theatres. The IDF experience suggests that more focus should be given to the area of ground warfare, which has a critical impact on the operational effectiveness of the IDF as a whole.

Other issues which bear consideration are:

- *Hezbollah's performance*. Hezbollah's operations against the IDF, focused on trying to inflict as many casualties as possible, were based on using prepared fixed posts. This is probably one of the first times that such a defensive tactic was used in a decentralised methodical manner. In most cases the organisation's fighting force did not carry out operational manoeuvres and when IDF troops came into direct contact with Hezbollah fighters, the IDF gained the upper hand. The effectiveness of the use of anti-tank weapons by Hezbollah was not unusual. The IDF's armoured forces could contend with such weapons successfully, by implementing their current weapon systems and doctrine. Underground fortifications and bunkers systems are mostly effective against approaching forces manoeuvring in killing zones. Swift penetration into these Hezbollah posts and direct close-range engagement of the enemy exposes the weakness of these positions. Efforts should be made to develop tactics that utilise this weakness.

- *Coordinating force build-up by the General Staff.* The IDF's force build-up processes have enormous impact on the preparedness of the fighting forces. Such processes do not only relate to the IDF's weapon systems procurement. Force build-up includes additional components such as: commanders' selection procedures, training, and the development of proper doctrines. The findings about the inadequate coordination between the air force and ground forces in the combined forces battle and in close air support, demands integration among the different services and branches. It must construct the interface among the different headquarters responsible for build-up processes to enable each to take into account the needs of the others.
- *Force build-up of the army (ground forces).* The negative phenomena observed in the army during the war resulted from processes that took place over many years, e.g. the lack of professionalism of some of the forces in conducting combined arms battles. Another key area that requires attention relates to the processes of selection, training, education, and instruction of the commanders.
- *The effectiveness of the independent ground forces headquarters.* The number of Israeli army divisions had significantly decreased over the past decade, while the resources for the ground forces headquarters had increased. The interface between the regional commands that actually command these fighting forces and the ground forces' headquarters that are responsible for the build-up of the force must be improved in order to better prepare the divisions' readiness for combat. The results of the different battles in this war showed that there is no correlation between the size of the ground forces' headquarters and the operational effectiveness of the fighting combat units.
- *Special forces.* The use of special forces in the war in Lebanon was not comprehensive enough. Their use in the fighting north of the Litani River as well as in Hezbollah's strategic rear were highly effective. However, the use of special operations by the Northern Command and even by the divisional level was inadequate. The need of a dedicated headquarters for the special forces and through improvement of regional and division commands capabilities to implement special operations was highlighted.
- *The time dimensions.* In the war, the time dimension comprised an important parameter. The messages conveyed by the political

leadership to the IDF indicated that Israel enjoyed legitimacy for its military operation, and therefore the IDF had no political time limit for realising the operational objectives. This message penetrated through IDF command echelons and harmed the forces' ability to execute their missions effectively and vigorously based on the notion that one should not put the forces at risk to attain an objective that might be achieved later with fewer casualties. Shortening the duration of the fighting is an operational need of the fighting force. The erosion of the time constraints lead eventually to a decline in the operational effectiveness of the forces. Despite the fact that the political leadership allowed the IDF a generous time frame, the IDF's forces had to understand that that it was incumbent on them to operate vigorously, aim to achieve their missions as quickly as possible, and shorten the duration of the war.

Ground Forces Operations

Four divisions operated in the Northern Command during the war. They were assembled incrementally during the course of the fighting, and were used in major operations only in the last days of the war. The Northern Command operated these divisions for two main efforts:

(a) At the beginning of the fighting the division that was already deployed along the border was given responsibility for all operations along the border. As the fighting developed the area of responsibility was divided between two divisions and eventually a third division was deployed along the most eastern part of the border.

(b) A deep manoeuvring effort was exercised only during the last days of the war and by one reserve division. This deep effort was designed to deal more effectively with Hezbollah's short-range rocketry.

Various insights can be derived from the ground operations:

- ***Lack of professionalism***. During the war inadequate professionalism of the forces and commanders in some of the combat units was observed. This was the case for regular as well as reserve units. Prior to the war most of the regular forces were engaged in combating Palestinian terror. When they were transferred to Lebanon, they were unfit to conduct combined forces battles integrating infantry, armour, engineer, artillery, and other support forces. In some instances, the units lacked both the skills and the necessary organic weapon systems required for this type of fighting. Units found themselves trying to adjust rapidly—often successfully—while engaged in fighting. The professionalism of the reserve troops was not better but for different reasons. It resulted from a years-long process during which the army reserves were neglected. The education and training of the officers were shown to be ineffective. The lack of practical training during reserve duty was evident, as was the lack of cohesion of the units, which had a detrimental effect on their operational capability.

- ***Combined forces warfare***. This is a fundamental element of ground-based fighting. Its nature stems from the combat force's ability to utilise the full range of combat capabilities: armour, infantry, reconnaissance, intelligence, engineers, artillery, standoff fire, electronic warfare, attack helicopters, and fighter bombers, as well as use of combat transport helicopter for deep operations in the enemy's rear and along the flanks. All these are supported by appropriate command and control abilities. The IDF's combat approach required an integration of all abilities in order to create the best mix for engaging in combat within various areas, to allow the achievement of the force's military objectives. Neglecting the use of some of these basic elements results in dysfunction of the combined force and impacts on the force's ability to complete its missions.

- ***Command issues***. Command of the battles in Lebanon was implemented by division commanders who had forces of various sizes under their command. Most of the commanders did not have the skills and training needed to operate a combined force professionally. A lack of knowledge in operating tank and infantry units was evident, and in some cases, engineer forces were not directed according to the IDF's doctrine. The artillery forces fired mostly on pre-planned targets and provided only inadequate close support for the ground forces. The available logistical systems were used only partially by the commanders, and this created supply problems and in a few instances required some units to exit the battlefield to obtain supplies. The lack of professionalism of some of the commanders in conducting combined forces battles ultimately led to situations in which units did not carry out their missions.

- ***Dysfunction of basic elements in combined operation***. The field commanders were not solely responsible for the inadequacy in operating the full combined force. For example: one of the most important tools of the fighting force is the capability to use close air support. The essence of such support is the ability of the commander to obtain aerial firepower against targets that were not pre-planned, in response to a changing operational situation. In practice, the air force approached this subject completely differently and interpreted the concept of close air support as another version of attacks on given ground targets. Another example of the failure to use combined assets was the lack of use of combat transport helicopters for transport of ground forces other than special operations. Thus, an important manoeuvring component was not used. The entire transport helicopter unit was set aside to serve the needs of special operations deep inside Lebanon, and did not at all support the forward division's operational needs.

- ***Simplicity of operational plans***. The ability to formulate an operational plan that is clear and simple is a basic component of the military art. Simplicity is a valuable element in a unit's ability to understand and ultimately carry out its mission effectively. In many cases and particularly among the regular force units, unclear orders were issued that were not based on formal IDF doctrine and were worded in unclear terminology. The origin of this lapse lies in thinking that became common in the IDF that there is a "magical operational solution," which once found and realised is bound to lead to victory. The main idea was to target the enemy's consciousness in ways that will make it possible to avoid direct engagement of the enemy in difficult battles. Military history, however, has repeatedly shown that battles are actual physical occurrences, and ultimately do not take place in the enemy's consciousness. Against any enemy, one has to achieve real results such as occupying territory, killing enemy fighters, blocking axes of movement, and so on.
- ***Frequent changes in the operational plans***. This phenomenon occurred too frequently among the ground forces. Changes are part of the art of battle, yet their frequency often affects the capability of carrying out a mission. In the war in Lebanon numerous changes were made, both in the articulation of missions and in the composition of the forces. These changes generated continual confusion at subordinate levels, which had a detrimental effect on the units' abilities to fight effectively and ultimately impacted negatively on their ability to fulfil

the missions. This phenomenon was a direct result of the lack of professionalism of some of the officers who while trying to achieve the "optimum" operational plan were not aware of the confusion caused by frequent changes that impairs execution of the mission.

- ***Continuity of fighting***. An important principle of fighting entails maintaining ongoing contact with and engagement of the enemy to prevent the latter from recovering, regrouping, and improving its situation. During the fighting in Lebanon this principle was noticeably absent from the thinking of commanders, resulting in intervals in the fighting and boosting the ability of the Hezbollah fighters to regroup and act against the IDF forces. The common explanation that this phenomenon is an offshoot of years of combating Palestinian terror in which the principle of avoidance of losses was a major priority provides only a partial answer, as some of the reserve units did not put this principle of war into practice despite not being involved in fighting Palestinian terror in recent years. This phenomenon was part of the broader lack of professionalism and training.

Special Forces Operations

Special operations are a significant tool available to military commanders, i.e., using a small force in order to strike the enemy deep in its rear. This is sometimes a clandestine operation, aimed at intelligence gathering, and sometimes it is a noisy raid. Using special forces deep in enemy territory is required on various levels in accordance with operational needs. It requires adequate professional skills, both of the operational force and of the commanding HQ.

The use of IDF special forces in Lebanon occurred mainly in the strategic depth of the enemy territory, and less in the areas closer to the battlefront. After the war broke out a post of coordinator for special operations was created in the Operations Branch of the General Staff for this purpose. The special operations activity in the Northern Command theatre sector was scarce and this was apparently a result of the lack of proficiency of the territorial command in carrying out special operations while simultaneously managing fighting in the front. Strategic special operations cannot replace the ones that the command has to implement to support its operational needs.

Special operations deep in enemy territory are highly effective in operational terms. Realising their potential requires enhancement of the command capability. In this context, two aspects merit consideration:

- *The need to establish an operational command for special operations, under the authority of the chief of staff.* This command will operate in addition to the existing eight operational commands of the IDF. It will be able to enhance the chief of staff's ability to control these operations as well as the flexibility of use of the special forces. The command has to be responsible for build-up of special forces capabilities as well as commanding them in war time.
- *Enhancing the capability of the regional command to carry out special operations.* This requires development of doctrine, organisation, and training.

International Action and Reaction

The governments of the United States, United Kingdom, Germany, Australia, and Canada asserted Israel's right to self-defence. The US government further responded by authorising Israel's request for expedited shipment of precision-guided bombs, but did not announce the decision publicly. US President George W. Bush said he thought the conflict was part of the "War on Terrorism". On 20 July 2006, the United States Congress voted overwhelmingly to support Israel's "right to defend itself".

Among neighbouring Middle Eastern nations, Iran, Syria, and Yemen voiced strong support for Hezbollah, while the Arab League, Egypt, and Jordan issued statements criticising Hezbollah's actions and declaring support for Lebanon. Saudi Arabia found Hezbollah entirely responsible. Egypt, Jordan, Kuwait, Iraq, the Palestinian Authority, the United Arab Emirates and Bahrain agreed with the Saudi stance that Hezbollah's actions were unexpected, inappropriate and irresponsible.

Several foreign governments organised the evacuation of their citizens from Lebanon. Many worldwide protests and demonstrations appealed for an immediate ceasefire and expressed concern for the heavy loss of civilian life on all sides. Other demonstrations were held exclusively in favour of Lebanon or Israel. Numerous newspaper advertising campaigns, SMS and email appeals, and online petitions also occurred.

Ceasefire

Terms for a ceasefire had been drawn and revised several times over the course of the conflict, yet successful agreement between the two sides took several weeks. Hezbollah maintained the desire for an unconditional ceasefire, while Israel insisted upon a conditional ceasefire, including the return of the two seized soldiers. Lebanon frequently pleaded for the United Nations Security Council to call for an immediate, unconditional ceasefire between Israel and Hezbollah. The US and UK, with support from several Arab leaders, delayed the ceasefire process. Outsider efforts to interfere with a ceasefire only ended when it became apparent Hezbollah would not be easily defeated.

On 11 August 2006, the United Nations Security Council unanimously approved UNSCR 1701, in an effort to end the hostilities. It was accepted by the Lebanese government and Hezbollah on 12 August 2006, and by the Israeli government on 13 August 2006. The ceasefire took effect at 0800 hours on 14 August 2006.

Before the ceasefire, the two Hezbollah members of the Lebanese cabinet said that their militia would not disarm south of the Litani River. Israel said it would stop withdrawing from Southern Lebanon if Lebanese troops were not deployed there within a matter of days.

Was the War Really a Victory for Hezbollah?

The Second Lebanon War ended indecisively and left Israel and Hezbollah to lick their wounds and draw their respective relevant conclusions. While the Israeli public had an uneasy sense of despondency and resorted to introspective self-castigation as to why Israel was unable to achieve the quick and decisive victory that many expected, the Hezbollah and its supporters revelled in their joy, with mass victory gatherings held in Syria and Lebanon.

Hezbollah's victory celebrations flaunted the organisation's ability to inflict continuous damage deep inside Israel and bring routine life in northern Israel to a standstill; kill Israeli civilians and soldiers; and maintain the ability to continue fighting, despite Israel's massive attack on its activists and infrastructures. Yet as with other guerrilla and terror organisations around the world, Hezbollah has in part earned an image of victory due to the difficulty in identifying the victors in confrontations that take place between states and sub-state organisations.

At the end of the fighting it seemed that the clash between Israel and Hezbollah was temporarily suspended but not over. Despite failures in the military campaign, Israel ensured that Hezbollah positions on its northern border were destroyed and its armed and entrenched personnel were no longer in prominent and provocative positions along the border.

The Lebanese army deployed forces in the south, thereby implementing UN resolutions 1559 and 1701, and a reinforced multinational force has been stationed in Lebanon near the border. However, Israel's faith in these forces' ability to restrain Hezbollah and prevent it from returning its personnel to villages in the south and rearming itself is highly limited. Hezbollah can boast that the heavy losses it sustained did not prevent it from continuing to fight and strike at Israel, and in its view, it emerged from the war as the victor. Even though it was forced to agree to deployment of the Lebanese army in the south of the country and the presence of a reinforced multinational force in Lebanon, to which it objected before the war, it considers this a tactical constraint and not a limitation that cannot be overcome if it decides to renew the confrontation with Israel. Hezbollah claims that its deterrence capability against Israel has not been damaged and may even have increased, as Israel discovered that in order to defeat Hezbollah it would have to pay a heavy price for any damage inflicted on the organisation in the future. Accordingly, Hezbollah feels it has sufficient room in which to manoeuvre and exploit the lack of a decisive conclusion to the war, and thereby resort to military power in the future as it sees fit.

Thus, in the post-confrontation reality, there is limited reciprocal deterrence between Israel and Hezbollah. This is based on the sides' understanding that a renewal of the hostilities now or in the near future is liable to demand of both parties a high and undesirable price, on the internal national level and international level. However, one of the clearest conclusions to be drawn from the 2006 war is that events of a localised and tactical nature and inaccurate assessments by both sides may cause the situation to deteriorate within a short time into another round of violence, even if the sides do not wish it.

Both sides to the conflict, Israel and Hezbollah, made announcements following the war, underlining their victory and success. Israeli Prime Minister Ehud Olmert was quick to underline the success and achievements of his country at the end of the war. Olmert argued that with Hezbollah pushed back from Israel's northern border, hundreds of its fighters dead and its headquarters in south Beirut battered, Israel was largely successful in achieving its goals. However, not everyone agreed in Israel.

Olmert was criticised for not being able to prevent Hezbollah's rocket attacks to Israel during the war. Northern Israel received a daily dose of 150-200 rockets a day, leading to the question of the ability of Israel to provide security for its own citizens. Besides, for many in Israel there was the image of their country being defeated by a group of terrorists, without a regular army.

Hezbollah, rather than being marginalised in Lebanon, increased its popularity and support not only in the country but also in the region at large. The results of a survey carried out after the war in Lebanon revealed that a majority of Lebanese believed that Hezbollah emerged as the biggest winner. Not only in Lebanon but in the Arab world at large, Hezbollah's popularity increased as a result of the war. After the War, Hezbollah leader Nasrallah was also quick to declare his own victory. Considering that the aim of the organisation was defined narrowly as survival during the war, they were successful in this limited aim. But whether this was a 'victory' is contested by many. Nasrallah underlined that it was a "strategic, historic, divine victory" in the Arab history. Considering that Hezbollah declared its aim during the war as survival and resistance to Israeli military forces, they were successful.

The war between Israel and Hezbollah has been hailed as a major turning point in the region, heralding the demise of Israel's military superiority and the rise of Hezbollah as the first Arab military organisation able to inflict a serious defeat on the IDF. The war will be studied for a long time and on several levels from the military-technical to the strategic and political. Because multiple narratives of the war will be written, one by Hezbollah and its supporters and at least several by Israelis, and because much of what happened will remain secret, various interpretations of the conflict will remain in discussion and important issues likely will continue in dispute.

Strategic Assessment

Prior to the Second Lebanon War, three relatively recent events had influenced Israeli expectations about the future of warfare:

- The war in Kosovo (1999) and initial US operations in Afghanistan (2001–2003) and Iraq (2003) revealed the implications of the revolution in military affairs, particularly in the areas of intelligence, surveillance, and reconnaissance, and precision strike. These implications fostered a belief among some in the Israeli defence establishment that standoff attack (principally by air power) was an effective means of affecting the will of the adversary and determining conflict outcomes. Standoff attack also seemed to promise lower IDF casualties (a major domestic political consideration), less collateral damage (a key consideration for managing international and regional opinion), and cost savings.

- The beginning of the Second *Intifada* (2000–2006) forced the Israeli Army to focus on operations designed to stop terrorist attacks inside Israel, and a mindset of low-intensity conflict developed. Further, significant budget issues curtailed IDF training.
- The US presence in Iraq after the end of major combat operations there, coupled with the low-level of threat to Israel posed by its neighbours (except Syria), encouraged Israelis to believe that, for them, the era of major wars had passed and that the role of ground forces was to carry out low-intensity irregular war.

The mindsets of Israel's military and political leaders were fundamentally, and understandably, shaped by these views. Defence spending was cut, armoured-unit training (deemed largely irrelevant in LIC) was neglected, the IDF staffs and processes responsible for integrating air and ground operations were removed from brigades, and there was little training in air-ground integration. The IDF, and particularly the active Israeli Army, focused on stopping terrorist attacks; indeed, the IDF was very successful in suppressing the Second *Intifada* and dramatically reducing Israeli casualties.

However, the Israeli Army's almost exclusive focus on LIC resulted in a military that was generally incapable of executing the integrated joint air-ground-ISR operations associated with major combat. Unfortunately for the Israelis, the Second Lebanon War (2006) demonstrated that taking a defended position from a hybrid force that is armed with standoff fires (e.g., ATGMs, mortars, MANPADS, rockets) requires forces trained and organised for integrated fire and manoeuvre tactics, however reduced in scale (compared with major combat operations) the size of that hybrid force might be. The role of air and ground power across the levels of adversary capabilities is at Table 8.

Ground Power vis-a-vis Adversary Capabilities

In conventional combat operations, troop deployment is a key signal of national commitment; combined-arms operations are the key to success; their employment forces an operational reaction from the enemy. Ground power engages ground units that avoid air attacks and indirect fire and are critical for exploiting operational opportunities and pursuing enemy forces. Ground forces are the best to deal with hybrid or irregular threats and are critical to establishing security and stability and are the best option to conduct decentralised operations against dispersed adversaries, in high-intensity major combat operations. The rules of engagement for ground forces can be tight and controlled.

Air Power vis-a-vis Adversary Capabilities

In major combat operations air power is critical to deterrence achieved through global reach and strike capabilities; ISR and signals intelligence are tightly linked with precision strike operations; air and space superiority may be contested at all levels; and centralised control is critical. Air power precludes large-scale ground manoeuvre by the enemy; air bases may be contested and operations may occur in a nuclear, biological, or chemical environment.

In the case of state-sponsored hybrid warfare air power is critical to attacking the enemy's deep strike assets and high-value targets; tight rules of engagement for centralised strikes and close air support are required; air power can be used for the suppression of enemy standoff systems to support (complement) ground manoeuvre denying the enemy's ability to concentrate and be reinforced. Air superiority may be contested below 20,000 feet.

In a counter-insurgency environment air mobility is critical to supply and evacuation, air power could be used mostly in ground-directed close air support with tight rules of engagement. It is also possible to be employed for force protection in extreme circumstances. Air superiority could be contested below 3,000 feet. Above 3,000 feet, air power is mainly invulnerable.

Lessons and Recommendations

The ultimate lesson from the Israeli experience in Lebanon is that an enemy's capabilities will largely determine the war a nation will have to fight. The imperative to conduct protracted low-intensity operations in Iraq and Afghanistan with limited ground forces has required the US to make choices about training focus and combat preparation that have diminished the readiness of US military forces to prevail against a hybrid enemy. In particular, the skills and processes required for integrated air-ground-ISR operations need to be assessed and strengthened. To that end, the key implications from the Israeli experience in Lebanon are:

- Despite the smaller scale of the conflict, hybrid opponents as Hezbollah constitute a challenge that is qualitatively similar to that posed by major combat operations because of their training, discipline, organisation, command and control, and effective standoff weapons. These capabilities are game changers. Irregular opponents who attain them can rapidly ratchet up the intensity level of a conflict, and defeating these opponents requires different skills than those used in counterinsurgency operations.
- There are no single-service solutions to the challenges posed by hybrid adversaries. Israel's training, organisational, and doctrinal changes after the Second Lebanon War, and particularly changes in air-ground-ISR integration, paid off in Operation *Cast Lead* for the IDF.
- Precision standoff fires were critical to—but not sufficient for— coping with hybrid opponents in Lebanon and Gaza, particularly when Israel's adversaries were operating among the population. Thus, as the IDF realised, joint, combined-arms operations are crucial in finding, fixing, and capturing or killing hybrid adversaries who are dispersed and concealed in complex terrain.
- Hybrid opponents become more visible when they take over and move into government buildings; this makes them more susceptible to precision strike. Similarly, intermediate- and long-range rockets are easier to find and destroy because of their size and the requirement that they be launched from relatively open sites. Thus, the IAF was very successful in finding and destroying intermediate- and long-range rockets and in attacking infrastructure targets. This is a unique capability afforded by air power, and it was particularly important in pre-empting the use of more-capable rockets. Additionally, only fixed-wing aircraft were capable of delivering precision ordnance with the payloads necessary to destroy large, multi-storey structures and tunnels.

- Persistent ISR coverage is crucial in tracking mobile opponents (particularly mortar, rocket, and ATGM crews) and high-value targets (e.g., intermediate- and long-range rockets in Lebanon, key enemy leaders). UAVs are particularly valuable because of their loitering time and because using unmanned (rather than manned) aircraft in high-threat environments eliminates the risk of losing a pilot. The ability to command and control a combination of ground forces, fixed-wing aircraft, attack helicopters, UAVs, and other assets—all operating off a "common picture" of the battlefield—is critical in attacking fleeting, time-sensitive targets and in avoiding collateral damage.
- Highly dispersed, low-signature targets (e.g., short-range rockets, ATGMs) are difficult to find and attack by air-only means, and attacking them requires comprehensive air-ground-ISR integration at low (i.e., battalion and brigade) levels; common references (e.g., detailed maps and control measures); and a shared, real-time ISR picture.
- Successfully striking targets, amongst the people, requires a combination of exquisite interagency intelligence, precision strike, and low-yield weapons. These capabilities are needed to identify targets, warn civilians, attack hidden targets (e.g., weapons caches, rockets) and avoid killing the wrong people.
- Armoured forces based on tanks and armoured personnel carriers are key elements of any force that will fight hybrid enemies with a modicum of training, organisation, effective standoff weapons, IEDs, and mines. Armoured forces reduce operational risks and minimise friendly casualties. Information cannot replace armour.

Taxonomy

"Irregular", guerrilla, or "asymmetric" warfare has usually been treated as a sharp dichotomy with conventional or "combined arms" warfare in military professional debates. Many of the differences are variations of degree rather than kind, and even differences of kind do not readily sort themselves into a handful of neat, categorical definitions. An intention to hold ground, for example, is commonly associated with conventional warfare. Guerrillas, by contrast, are typically assumed to favour hit-and-run methods in which retention of ground is not attempted and in which the guerrillas' orientation is to the enemy, not the terrain per se. The classical guerrilla chooses terrain based solely on its potential to inflict casualties, not for its control. Guerrillas are expected to melt away when attacked by superior government forces rather than to stand their ground and accept decisive engagement, and they often prefer booby traps, mines, roadside bombs, or harassing rocket or mortar fire meant to inflict casualties without denying the opponent access to an area per se.

Concealment is another trait often held to distinguish conventional from guerrilla warfare. Concealment is typically seen as critical for guerrilla forces, which depend on this for survival in the face of superior government militaries. Yet even in conventional warfare, exposure frequently means death. Contrasts in strategic intent are another distinction often drawn between guerrilla and conventional warfare.

The key distinctions are differences of degree not kind. Thus, the difference between "guerrilla" and "conventional" war making cannot be considered a dichotomy, but as a continuum of conflict.

CONCLUSION

The war between the IDF and the Lebanese Shia militia Hezbollah is a harbinger of future wars in the Middle East and other parts of the world. Unlike conventional war, it saw the most powerful army in the Middle East battling against a popularly-supported militant movement. What distinguishes this war is the question of feasibility that arises over the use of conventional warfare against an insurgent group relying heavily on guerrilla warfare and religious convictions.

What distinguishes Hezbollah from a regular army is its manipulation of the fragmented reality in Lebanon. For a long time, South Lebanon was abandoned to the leadership of feudal politicians who did not care much about the fate of the local population. Hezbollah played on the weakness of the central government in Beirut and the alienation that the PLO had created throughout its years of military operations against Israel, to become a major military and political actor in Lebanese politics. The question is how do you deal with a terrorist group that has popular backing? Hezbollah is undeniably an important element in Lebanon's politics, although its influence continues to be a malign one. The movement will realistically only be disarmed through a political process.

From a military perspective, the June 2006 war has led to a major rethink in Israeli war-making. One of the major stumbling blocks of the Israeli operation in Lebanon was its failure to identify and pinpoint Hezbollah's military positions and movements. The other shortfall was the lack of military preparation. Lessons to be learned include:

(a) You cannot defeat an insurgent group that has popular backing.

(b) To isolate Hezbollah, you have to strengthen the central government in Lebanon and bring in moderate Shia leaders that are currently excluded from the political process.

(c) The integration of Hezbollah militias into the Lebanese Armed Forces needs to be encouraged.

(d) Waging another war against Hezbollah could lead to more destruction and the end of Lebanon as a state. Partition of Lebanon into various sectarian territories will not solve the problem.

The Israel-Lebanon war defined a new pattern of warfare in the Middle East, in which the military confrontation represented not only the warring parties—in this case, Israel and Hezbollah—but, rather, three levels of confrontation encompassed in a single theatre of operations.

(a) The war constituted another episode of the Arab-Israeli conflict. It reflected the general law of Arab-Israeli politics: that unless progress is made in Arab-Israeli peace-making, violence in one manner or another will eventually erupt.

(b) The post-September 11 world has made the vacuum in peace-making all the more pronounced. This war was also an expression of Lebanese domestic politics and an extension of the Lebanese civil war. The Ta'if Agreement that formally ended the Lebanese civil war in 1989 had stipulated the disarming of all Lebanese militias; and all the militias disarmed with the exception of Hezbollah, which not only remained armed but also maintained a monopoly of force in all of South Lebanon and in parts of Beirut. The balance of power in Lebanese politics changed after the Syrians withdrew, and Hezbollah apparently thought that nothing would restore the balance better than a war with Israel. The Lebanese people were thus presented with an unpalatable choice: a war with Israel or another bloody civil war.

(c) The war can also be understood as part of the broader US war on terror—or, even more generally, on fundamentalist Islam. The post-September 11 war on terror has expanded to different parts of the globe. The war launched by Hezbollah, on 12 July 2006, and its subsequent perceived victory were part of the Islamic counter-offensive. The Arab-Israeli dimension of the war was not different in kind from other episodes in the historical sequence of wars over the past six decades. However, the global dimension of the Israel-Lebanon war has made it central to the conduct of regional politics and international relations and the best manner of dealing with radical and fundamentalist Islam.

On 27 August 2006, Nasrallah said in an interview with New TV that the abduction of the two soldiers did not cause the war. It only advanced a long-planned war for a few months. But he added: "If there was even a one percent chance that the 11 July capturing operation would have led to a war like the one that happened, would you have done it? I would say no, absolutely not, for humanitarian, moral, social, security, military, and political reasons. [...] What happened is not an issue of a reaction to a capturing operation... what happened was already planned for. The fact that it happened in July has averted a situation that would have been a lot worse, had the war been launched in October." On 22 September 2006, some eight hundred thousand Hezbollah supporters gathered in Beirut for a rally at which Nasrallah stated that Hezbollah had achieved a "divine and strategic victory."

Within hours of Israeli's bombing of Lebanon, on 13 July 2006, hundreds of protesters gathered in Tel Aviv to oppose the war. On 22 July, about 2,000 people, including many Palestinian Arab citizens of Israel, demanded an end to the offensive during a protest march in Tel Aviv's Rabin Square. By 25 August, 63 percent of Israelis polled wanted Olmert to resign due to his handling of the war. The *Jerusalem Post* said that " if you fail to win, you lose" and that as "Hezbollah survived, it won the war."

Prime Minister Olmert of Israel admitted to the Knesset that there were mistakes in the war in Lebanon, though he framed UNSCR 1701 as an accomplishment for Israel that would bring home the captured soldiers, and said that the operations had altered the regional strategic balance vis-à-vis Hezbollah. The Israeli Chief of Staff, Dan Halutz, admitted to failings in the conflict. On 15 August, Israeli government and defence officials called for Halutz's resignation following a stock scandal in which he admitted selling stocks hours before the start of the Israeli offensive. Halutz subsequently resigned on 17 January 2007.

Israel's war against Hezbollah was indeed marked by a long series of failures. On 11 October 2006, retired justice Eliyahu Winograd was appointed as chair of a governmental commission—the Winograd Commission to inquire into the circumstances and events of the war. According to the Commission report, the Second Lebanon War was a missed opportunity and that Israel initiated a long war, which ended without a defined military victory. The report stated that a semi-military organisation of a few thousand men resisted, for a few weeks, the strongest army in the Middle East, which enjoyed full air superiority and size and technology advantages. Furthermore, Hezbollah's rocket attacks continued throughout the war and the IDF did not provide an effective response to it. Following a long period of using standoff firepower and limited ground activities, the IDF launched a large-scale ground offensive close to the UN Security Council's resolution which imposed a cease-fire. This offensive did not result in military gains and was not completed.

A decision was made on the night of 12 July to react (to the capturing of Israeli soldiers) with immediate and substantive military action and to set ambitious goals. This decision had immediate repercussions in that subsequent decisions were limited mainly to a choice between (a) a short, painful and unexpected blow on Hezbollah and (b) to bring about a significant change of the reality in the South of Lebanon with a large ground operation, occupying the South of Lebanon and 'cleaning' it of Hezbollah. The fact that Israel went to war before it decided which option to select and without an exit strategy, constituted serious failures of the decision-making process. As for achievements, the Commission reported that UNSCR 1701, and the fact that it was adopted unanimously, were an achievement for Israel.

Hezbollah may have won the propaganda war, but on the ground, it lost badly. Hezbollah's entrenched infrastructure along Israel's border was shattered and cannot be easily rebuilt due to the presence of the Lebanese Army and a robust UNIFIL force. Hundreds of Hezbollah's best fighters were killed in the war, and many Lebanese were angry with Hezbollah for provoking a war which largely devastated the country. Yet, though outgunned and outnumbered, Hezbollah managed to hold off Israel's advanced armed forces and proved its ability to damage Israel by launching rockets at its territory until the end of the war. Hezbollah's destructive capabilities have increased in the years after the war and it is capable of inflicting far worse damage on the Israeli home front than in 2006. It is clear that any future combat with Hezbollah will be very bloody and Lebanon would suffer heavy damage.

In the days following the 14 August 2006 ceasefire, Hezbollah launched dozens of rockets and mortars inside southern Lebanon, which Israel did not respond to, though there were several instances where Israeli troops killed armed Hezbollah members approaching their positions. Israeli warplanes continued conducting numerous flyovers and manoeuvres above southern Lebanon, which Israel said did not violate the ceasefire. On 19 August 2006, Israel launched a raid in Lebanon's eastern Beqaa Valley aimed at disrupting Hezbollah's weapons supply from Syria and Iran.

On 7 September 2006 and 8 September 2006 respectively, aviation and naval blockades were lifted. In the second half of September, Hezbollah claimed victory and asserted an improvement in their position, and they redeployed to some positions on the border as Israel completed its withdrawal from Lebanon, save border-straddling Ghajar.

On 16 July 2008, in accordance with the mandates of UNSCR 1701, Hezbollah transferred the coffins of captured Israeli soldiers, Ehud Goldwasser and Eldad Regev, in exchange for incarcerated Palestine Liberation Front militant Samir Kuntar, four Hezbollah militants captured by Israel during the war, and bodies of about 200 other Lebanese and Palestinian militants held by Israel. Until that time, Hezbollah had provided no information on Goldwasser and Regev's condition and disallowed the Red Cross from visiting them.

The Lebanese still have to reach a final agreement on three basic issues:

(a) The viability of the Ta'if Accords and whether they are still applicable in the current situation, especially in light of the changes brought about by the 2006 war;

(b) The role Lebanon should play in the Israeli-Palestinian conflict; and

(c) Whether Lebanon should implement economic policies reflecting a situation of war or peace.

From these developments, most Arab states drew a number of conclusions vis-à-vis Israel. First, Israel has overall strategic superiority over the Arab states and as such, the Arab armies are unable, in the foreseeable future, to defeat it on the battlefield and destroy it as a political entity. This conclusion derives from the assumption that Israel is militarily stronger than each individual Arab state and, apparently, than an entire Arab military coalition as well (which in any event the Arabs have been incapable of mobilising effectively). The central factors in Israel's superiority are its aerial strength, its quality intelligence, its ability to operate large ground formations, its advantage in the field of precision arms, its command and control systems, and its extended reach. The Arabs appear to believe that despite the advances in quality made in some Arab armies in the last two decades, particularly in the Egyptian army, the discrepancy between the IDF and the Arab armies has increased further in Israel's favour.

Second, Israel's strategic superiority results from the confluence of several factors: on the one hand, Israel's ability to develop and utilise its human resources and harness them for its defence needs; its ability to obtain advanced military technologies and weapon systems—some from American and Western sources, and some self-developed; and its ability to formulate and adopt advanced fighting methods and adapt them to the conditions of the Arab-Israeli arena. For their part, the Arabs have failed in most of these areas, and have not managed to harness their resources and unite to overcome their inferiority vis-à-vis Israel.

The special relationship between the US and Israel; the commitment of American administrations to Israel's survival and security; and the US commitment to maintain Israel's qualitative edge over the Arab states are among the pillars of Israeli security. These relations provide Israel not only with a source of technological superiority but also superpower backing in times of military distress during a war. The Arabs, however, have no such support in their confrontation with Israel.

Israel also has a strategic security net based on its nuclear capability. At the same time, the Arabs do not believe Israel will use nuclear weapons against them unless it finds itself in extreme distress and has no other option, which they do not think will happen in the foreseeable future. As such, the Arabs are of the opinion that Israel's nuclear capability should not limit or deter them from acting against it, either in a conventional war or through terror and violence. In addition, Israel has weak points that stem from its smaller geographical size and population, sensitivity to losses, political constraints, dependence of the IDF on reserve forces, and its difficulties in contending with terror and guerrilla organisations.

These factors oblige the Arabs to adopt strategic conclusions with regard to their approach towards Israel. Here, the Arabs are divided over what conclusions to draw. Today all the Arab regimes believe that embarking on another war with Israel in the coming years is not in their favour because they would inevitably be defeated. As such, their strategic interest is to solve the Arab-Israeli conflict by political means, while adhering to the objective of attaining the Arab demands. Egypt and Jordan translated this approach into peace agreements with Israel. Syria has looked for a political settlement, but has not achieved it due to the gap between Syrian and Israeli positions. Other Arab countries are divided between willingness to maintain informal relations with Israel and a refusal to have any ties with Israel at all. The Palestinians are divided in their approach: some are willing to accept a political compromise settlement with Israel that satisfies their basic conditions, while the radical organisations support maintaining the armed struggle until attrition achieves victory over Israel. The only regime in the region that supports an armed struggle against Israel until it is annihilated is the Iranian regime.

For over a generation the Arabs have noted Israel's inability to achieve all its military objectives. Israel is still considered by them as a threat due to its military ability and intentions to occupy Arab territory. However, in all wars since the Six Day War—the peak of Israel's realisation of its military abilities against the Arabs—the Arabs have uncovered weak points in Israel's strength: in the War of Attrition, the Yom Kippur War, the Lebanon War and the clash with Hezbollah, and the struggle against Palestinian terror. In Arab eyes, the war in Lebanon is, therefore, part of this general pattern.

Recourse to war as a means of solving international controversies was outlawed by the Pact of Paris (the Kellogg-Briand Pact) in 1928. It was also restricted by the Charter of the League of Nations drafted at the end of the Great War (1914-18). The Atlantic Charter, the UN Charter, and the Helsinki Final Act restricted the scope of state resort to armed force still further. The UN Charter provides in Article 2(4): "*All Members shall refrain in their international relations from the threat or use of force against the territorial integrity or political independence of any State, or in any other manner inconsistent with the Purposes of the United Nations.*"

Today, the prohibition of aggression is universally considered to have reached the status of a *jus cogens* norm. In fact, crimes associated with war entail individual criminal responsibility, and military commanders implicated in such atrocities can be indicted before the International Criminal Court in The Hague. Alternatively, they can be tried in the courts of third states under the doctrine of universal jurisdiction. This is relevant in the present situation since neither Israel nor Lebanon is a State Party to the Rome Statute.

To make a legitimate claim of self-defence under international law, reference must be made to Article 51 of the UN Charter which provides in part: "*Nothing in the present Charter shall impair the inherent right of individual or collective self-defence if an armed attack occurs against a Member of the United Nations, until the Security Council has taken measures necessary to maintain international peace and security."* Israel's UN Ambassador referenced Article 51, on 12 July 2006, in identical letters to the UN Secretary-General and the Security Council. He wrote:

> "Israel thus reserves the right to act in accordance with Article 51 of the Charter of the United Nations and exercise its right of self-defence when an armed attack is launched against a Member of the United Nations. The State of Israel will take the appropriate actions to secure the release of the kidnapped soldiers and bring an end to the shelling that terrorizes our citizens".

The Israeli version of events is that Hezbollah started the conflict by capturing two soldiers, killing several others, and firing a salvo of rockets into Israeli border villages on 14 July. Even so, it is not entirely clear whether Israel can claim a right of self-defence under the UN Charter. Israel can make a legitimate claim under Article 51 only if the attack by Hezbollah could be classified as an "armed attack" and not a mere frontier incident.

It also raises the question of whether non-state actors can be held culpable according to state practice. This opinion is moot. The fact that the G8 referred to Hezbollah specifically, rather than Lebanon, may be evidence of a new custom emerging. Nevertheless, whether Article 51 permits a state to defend itself in the event of an armed attack by a non-state actor is cognisable only if there is a certain link with a state.

While the attack of 12 July 2006 may not independently trigger Article 51, Israel could invoke the doctrine, known as the "accumulation of events theory." According to the doctrine, each specific act of terrorism, or needle prick, though it may not independently qualify as an armed attack, could, taking into consideration the totality of incidents, amount to an armed attack entitling the victim state to respond with armed force.

If Israel is permitted to invoke the afore-saidtheory, it could just as easily be used by Lebanon, for Israel frequently enters Lebanon's territorial waters without its consent. Furthermore, the Lebanese government accuses Israel of regularly violating its airspace between May 2000 and July 2006. Lebanon considers these incursions a form of international terrorism, alleging that these low-altitude flights break the sound barrier over civilian-populated areas and instil terror among Lebanese civilians, especially children.

Above all, nothing would justify Israel's war against Lebanon. The border had been relatively stable since Israel's withdrawal from southern Lebanon in 2000, although there were several clashes within the Blue Line (in Lebanon) in the Sha'ba Farms area. Yet Israel did not respond with such overwhelming force in its previous clashes with Hezbollah. One may question why Israel felt the need to respond so aggressively in July 2006. Regardless of the various theories advanced in support of military action, the use of force in international relations is subject to the conditions of proportionality and necessity. This means that a state may only use force that is necessary to repel an armed attack and its response must be proportional to that attack. After all, the whole *raison d'être* of the UN Charter is to "save succeeding generations from the scourge of war."

Hezbollah's 14 July attack on Israel did not threaten its territorial integrity or political independence, the only grounds for justifiable war. Rather, the converse is true: Israel's bombardment of Lebanon's major cities and its full-scale invasion of the south threatened its existence and political independence as a sovereign nation. Even if Israel could resort to Article 51—assuming that it was subject to an armed attack—it would seem that Israel exhausted that right when it pursued the guerrillas into Lebanon in the aftermaths of the initial attack. Israel's actions were neither necessary nor proportionate to the scale of the threat posed by Hezbollah. It is arguable whether the right of self-defence would be relevant to territory which is subject to belligerent occupation, particularly if it is prolonged and protracted. There are also sound reasons not to confuse border incidents with armed attacks.

APPENDICES

Appendix A

THE SHAB'A FARMS DISPUTE

Shab'a Farms, the hilly ridge that forms the western extension of Mount Hermon next to Israel's primary water source, appeared on the agenda after the IDF withdrawal from Lebanon in May 2000, and it re-emerged prominently during and after the Second Lebanon War. This arid area is on the southern slopes of Mount Hermon, south of the internationally recognised Syrian-Lebanese border and north-west of the Golan Heights, stretching south-west to north-east; the area is about three kilometres wide and 14 kilometres long, totalling about 40 square kilometres. The only settlement near the area is the village of Ghajar, divided by the "blue line" marked by the United Nations (UN; UN Resolution 425) in May 2000 into a Syrian part occupied by Israel and a Lebanese part.

The Lebanese Government has repeatedly demanded possession of Shab'a Farms, known in Israel as Mount Dov. Security Council Resolution 1701 explicitly includes it as an issue to be discussed in the context of relations between Lebanon and Israel and instructs the UN Secretary-General to submit to the Security Council recommendations for resolving the dispute. In addition, President Bashar Asad pointed out in a television interview, on 26 September 2006, that before all else, Israel must withdraw from Shab'a Farms; and in the Lebanese press there are public announcements from the Lebanese government calling for former residents of the farms to come forward and present their ownership papers.

1967-1999

Just before the end of hostilities in the Six-Day War the senior Israeli military echelon gathered at the headquarters of Division 36, which was responsible for the Golan Heights. Ezer Weizmann, then head of

Operations in the IDF, turned to Defence Minister Moshe Dayan and said: "Don't you think the air force deserves a reward?" "Certainly," answered Dayan, "ask for anything." At the time the IDF forces had advanced as far as the Druze village of Majdal Shams, in the foothills of Mt. Hermon. Weizmann pointed at Mt. Hermon and said: "I want us to have a position up there, the point from where you can see Damascus."

Where was that point? Everyone looked at the divisional intelligence officer, Danny Agmon, one of the founding fathers of IDF combat intelligence. Agmon sat down, calculated, measured the maps, and went up to the spot in a helicopter. Israeli soldiers followed, and on the next day UN personnel and a surveyor went to the spot to take measurements and mark the place on their maps as an IDF location. But then a problem arose: the line had to continue to the Lebanese border. In accordance with the "accepted" sign for an international border on the 1:100000 scale map of the intelligence officer, a number of soldiers were stationed on the prominent hilltops along the border. The UN personnel and surveyor came and noted the line of the IDF forces on their maps as following the line of the international border between Syria and Lebanon. The IDF later abandoned the area of the Syrian-Lebanese border.

In the early 1970s, however, Palestinian terrorists infiltrated the area, subsequently nicknamed "Fatahland." The IDF took possession of it, paved a road, and established a chain of positions there. The hill, called Jabal Rus, became known as Mt. Dov, named after Capt. Dov Rodberg who was killed there in August 1970 in a battle with terrorists. This is also the time when the farmers who lived there abandoned their homes, and ever since the farms have been unoccupied. After the Yom Kippur War and the signing of the disengagement treaty between Israel and the Syrians, the UN force (UNDOP) was established. The operational regional map naturally included Mt. Dov, based on the marking of the international border that a UN surveyor and Danny Agmon delineated in 1967.

2000-2006

Prime Minister Barak of Israel made the decision to withdraw from Lebanon without an agreement with Syria, in 2000. He determined that the withdrawal would take place as part of Security Council resolution 425, adopted following Operation Litani in 1978. According to this resolution, Israel was to withdraw to the international Israel-Lebanon border. UN envoy Terje Larsen was sent to Israel and Lebanon, together with a team of UN surveyors, in part to clarify the line to which IDF had to withdraw in order to comply with resolution 425. The main problem was the border with Lebanon, drawn in 1923—where exactly did it run? On the eastern border, from the Hatzbani River and eastwards, meaning the Lebanese-Syrian border, there were no special problems, except for two important IDF positions inside Lebanese territory.

In a meeting with Lebanese President Emile Lahoud, on 4 May 2000, Larsen and his team were told that the border with Israel did not interest him just then. The eastern border was far more important to Lebanon. He claimed that this area, which was called Shab'a Farms, was Lebanese and not Syrian, and Israel had to withdraw from it in accordance with resolution 425. Lahoud noted that at this location there were at least fourteen farms, the largest of them being Mizrat Shab'a (after which the region of the farms is named.

The Lebanese media, including Hezbollah's media and the speaker of the Lebanese parliament, Nabih Berri, immediately made this public. Larsen returned to Israel where a Lebanese map was shown to him with the accepted Lebanese-Syrian border, with Shab'a Farms clearly marked in Syrian territory. The Lebanese claimed that the map was not up-to-date and, in any case, was inaccurate, and insisted that the area of Shab'a Farms (without precisely denoting its boundaries) is located in Lebanon. From that moment and until the publication of a report by the UN secretary-general to the Security Council, on May 23, a struggle ensued over the position of the Syrian-Lebanese border and to whom Shab'a Farms belong: Syria or Lebanon. The UN asked Israel and Lebanon to provide evidence to support their claims, and launched an investigation of its own.

Two fundamental historic facts lay at the basis of the struggle: one, there was no formal agreement between Syria and Lebanon over a formal international border, and second, there was no agreed marking of the border. The actual border between Lebanon and Syria was set in 1920 by the French when the state of Lebanon was established.

The Lebanese had four arguments:

(a) Syrian property notes testify that the farms belong to the Lebanese.
(b) Various documents show that religious leaders from Lebanon provided the inhabitants of the farms with religious services.

(c) Partial minutes of a Lebanese-Syrian borders committee meeting from 1964 allegedly indicated that the Syrian side agreed that the farms belong to Lebanon, and the route of the border should be reset.

(d) One Lebanese map from 1966 shows the farms as being on Lebanese soil.

Israel clearly saw this as a Hezbollah pretext to fabricate an issue that would validate acts of violence after the IDF withdrawal, claiming that this is occupied Lebanese territory. The arguments Israel submitted to the UN to show that the area is Syrian and not Lebanese included:

(a) Dismissal of the Lebanese claim of a purchase certificate as being entirely irrelevant to the question of sovereignty.

(b) Showing proof that the so-called 1964 minutes, presented by the Lebanese, were in fact forged.

(c) Showing dozens of Lebanese maps printed after 1964, including from the Lebanese Ministry of Defence, that clearly indicate that the farms are located on Syrian soil.

(d) Syrian maps representing the same information.

(e) French maps were brought in, along with testimony of French officials who described where the border between Syria and the new state of Lebanon ran.

(f) A Syrian census from 1960 showed that the inhabitants of the farms were incorporated into a population census (this ranged from several dozen to several hundred at each farm).

(g) A Lebanese banknote with a value of 1000 Lebanese lira, which was issued in 1988 and which bears a map of Lebanon. The route of the Syrian-Lebanese border, marked out on the map, indicates that area of Shab'a Farms is, in fact, Syrian land.

(h) Maps belonging to UNDOP and UNIFIL, including their activity areas, are divided by the "accepted" line of the Syrian-Lebanese border.

(i) The UN announcement from 1978 (after Operation Litani) stated that Israel had completed its withdrawal from all Lebanese territory (without referring to IDF positions on Mt. Dov as belonging to Lebanon).

The UN accepted Israel's position and announced this to the Lebanese government several days after submission of the UN secretary-general's report to the Security Council on 23 May 2000. The UN's main reason for rejecting the Lebanese demand was connected to the UNDOP and UNIFIL maps. The UNDOP map appeared in the protocol of the disengagement agreement between Israel and Syria in May 1974, which Syria signed, thereby confirming that the area of Shab'a Farms is located in Syria, as part of the occupied Golan Heights; Lebanon never complained that UNIFIL's operational area does not include Shab'a Farms.

The Lebanese did not give up. They repeated their claim that the area is Lebanese and therefore the UN position is unacceptable. The Syrians supported the Lebanese and claimed then, and still do today, that the farms belong to the Lebanese. In terms of ownership the farms in fact belong to Lebanese.

On 20 May 2000, Nasrallah announced that Shab'a Farms is occupied Lebanese territory, thereby establishing the legitimacy for future violence against Israel. Syria was to sign an official border agreement with Lebanon, mark the border (according to which the farms would be in Lebanese territory) and initiate the accepted international processes pertaining to defining an international border (parliamentary approval, sending maps to the UN, and so on.) However, signing the border agreement with Lebanon meant that Syria would officially signify ceding part of the Golan Heights that had been occupied by Israel since 4 June 1967. It would create a precedent that would damage the fundamental Syrian position. Lebanon and Syria have thus not signed a binding international border agreement (in which sovereignty of the farms would be decided).

In 2005 the Syrians withdrew from Lebanon. The Un proposed that Israel vacate the area of Shab'a Farms and transfer it to the Lebanese government (or, initially, to the UN). There were two components to this rationale. First, this would obviate Hezbollah's grounds for firing on Israel and bring complete quiet to the northern border. Second, this would bolster the reformist forces in Lebanon (i.e., Prime Minister Siniora) against Hezbollah and add weight to the demand that Hezbollah disarm in accordance with UNSCR 1559. Israel rejected the idea outright, arguing that Shab'a Farms is not Lebanese territory. Mt. Dov is of supreme strategic importance to Israel as it controls the three water sources of the Jordan River (Dan, Hatzbani, and Banias), and in general, there is no precise and clear geographic delineation of Shab'a Farms.

The Shab'a Farms issue will undoubtedly remain on the political, diplomatic, and even military agenda in the future. There are five players in the issue: the UN, the Lebanese government, Hezbollah, Syria, and Israel.

The Shab'a Farms also represent an issue of significance far beyond the immediate local context. Apparently, the more Arab states conclude peace agreements with Israel, consequently eliminating grounds for conflict, the greater the salience of these arid farmlands, a colonial relic resurrected for twenty-first century purposes. It has been made the centre pillar of strategising Syrian and Iranian political interests in the region, tied in to water rights—and scarcity thereof—in the area, the Israeli-Palestinian conflict, Lebanese effective sovereignty, and Israel's security at large, and the stature of the UN.

Appendix B

FINAL REPORT OF THE COMMISSION TO INVESTIGATE THE LEBANON CAMPAIGN (THE WINOGRAD REPORT)

30 January 2008

Press Release

1. About an hour ago we submitted the Final Report of the Commission to Investigate the Lebanon Campaign in 2006 to the Prime minister, Mr. Ehud Olmert, and to the Minister of Defence, Mr. Ehud Barak.
2. The task given to us was difficult and complex. It involved the examination of events in 34 days of fighting, and the scrutiny of events before the war, since the IDF had left Lebanon in 2000. This covered extensive, charged and complex facts, unprecedented in any previous Commission of Inquiry.
3. The fact that the Government of Israel opted for such an examination, and that the army conducted a large number of inquiries of a variety of military events, are a sign of strength, and an indication that the political and military leaders of Israel are willing to expose themselves to critical review and to painful but required mending.
4. We have included in the classified version of the Report all the relevant facts we have found concerning the 2nd Lebanon war, systematically and in a chronological order. This presentation of the factual basis was an important part of our work. It is reasonable to assume that no single decision maker had access to a similar factual basis. In this task we had a unique advantage over others who have written about this war, since we had access to a lot of primary and comprehensive

material, and the opportunity to clarify the facts by questioning many witnesses, commanders and soldiers, including bereaved families.

5. For obvious reasons, the unclassified Report does not include the many facts that cannot be revealed for reasons of protecting the state's security and foreign affairs. We tried, nonetheless, to balance between the wish to present the public with a meaningful picture of the events and the needs of security. We should note that we did not take the mere fact that some data has already been published in the media as a reason for including it in our unclassified Report.

6. We, the members of the Commission, acted according to the main objectives for which the Commission was established—to respond to the bad feelings of the Israeli public of a crisis and disappointment caused by the results of the 2nd Lebanon war, and from the way it was managed by the political and military echelons; and the wish to draw lessons from the failings of the war and its flaws, and to repair what is required, quickly and resolutely. We regarded as most important to investigate deeply what had happened, as a key to drawing lessons for the future, and their implementation.

7. This conception of our role was one of the main reasons for our decision not to include in the Final Report personal conclusions and recommendations. We believe that the primary need for improvements applies to the structural and systemic malfunctioning revealed in the war—on all levels. Nonetheless, it should be stressed that the fact we refrained from imposing personal responsibility does not imply that no such responsibility exists. We also wish to repeat our statement from the Interim Report: We will not impose different standards of responsibility to the political and the military echelons, or to persons of different ranks within them.

8. Let us emphasise: when we imposed responsibility on a system, an echelon or a unit, we did not imply that the responsibility was only or mainly of those who headed it at the time of the war. Often, such responsibility stemmed from a variety of factors outside the control of those at the head. In addition, a significant part of the responsibility for the failures and flaws we have found lies with those who had been in charge of preparedness and readiness in the years before the war.

9. The purpose of this press release is not to sum up the Final Report.

Rather, it is to present its highlights. The Report itself includes discussions of many important issues, which are an inseparable part of the Report, its conclusions and recommendations.

10. In the Final Report we dealt mainly with the events of the period after the initial decision to go to war, which we had discussed in the Interim Report. Yet the events of the period covered by the Final Report took place under the shadow of the constraints created by the decision to go to war, with all its failings and flaws. We want to stress that we stand behind everything we said in the Interim Report, and the two parts of the Report complement each other.

11. Overall, we regard the 2nd Lebanon war as a serious missed opportunity. Israel initiated a long war, which ended without its clear military victory. A semi-military organisation of a few thousand men resisted, for a few weeks, the strongest army in the Middle East, which enjoyed full air superiority and size and technology advantages. The barrage of rockets aimed at Israel's civilian population lasted throughout the war, and the IDF did not provide an effective response to it. The fabric of life under fire was seriously disrupted, and many civilians either left their home temporarily or spent their time in shelters. After a long period of using only standoff fire power and limited ground activities, Israel initiated a large-scale ground offensive, very close to the Security Council resolution imposing a cease fire. This offensive did not result in military gains and was not completed. These facts had far-reaching implications for us, as well as for our enemies, our neighbours, and our friends in the region and around the world.

12. In the period we examined in the Final Report—from July 18, 2006, to August 14, 2006- again troubling findings were revealed, some of which had already been mentioned in the Interim Report:

- We found serious failings and shortcomings in the decision-making processes and staff-work in the political and the military echelons and their interface.
- We found serious failings and flaws in the quality of preparedness, decision-making and performance in the IDF high command, especially in the Army.
- We found serious failings and flaws in the lack of strategic thinking and planning, in both the political and the military echelons.

- We found severe failings and flaws in the defence of the civilian population and in coping with its being attacked by rockets.
- These weaknesses resulted in part from inadequacies of preparedness and strategic and operative planning which go back long before the 2nd Lebanon war.

13. The decision made in the night of July 12th—to react (to the kidnapping) with immediate and substantive military action, and to set for it ambitious goals—limited Israel's range of options. In fact, after the initial decision had been made, Israel had only two main options, each with its coherent internal logic, and its set of costs and disadvantages. The first was a short, painful, strong and unexpected blow on Hezbollah, primarily through standoff fire-power. The second option was to bring about a significant change of the reality in the South of Lebanon with a large ground operation, including a temporary occupation of the South of Lebanon and 'cleaning' it of Hezbollah military infrastructure.
14. The choice between these options was within the exclusive political discretion of the government; however, the way the original decision to go to war had been made; the fact Israel went to war before it decided which option to select, and without an exit strategy—all these constituted serious failures, which affected the whole war. Responsibility for these failures lay, as we had stressed in the Interim Report, on both the political and the military echelons.
15. After the initial decision to use military force, and to the very end of the war, this period of 'equivocation' continued, with both the political and the military echelon not deciding between the two options: amplifying the military achievement by a broad military ground offensive, or abstaining from such a move and seeking to end the war quickly. This 'equivocation' did hurt Israel. Despite awareness of this fact, long weeks passed without a serious discussion of these options, and without a decision—one way or the other—between them.
16. In addition to avoiding a decision about the trajectory of the military action, there was a very long delay in the deployment necessary for an extensive ground offensive, which was another factor limiting Israel's freedom of action and political flexibility: Till the first week of August, Israel did not prepare the military capacity to start a massive ground operation.

17. As a result, Israel did not stop after its early military achievements, and was 'dragged' into a ground operation only after the political and diplomatic timetable prevented its effective completion. The responsibility for this basic failure in conducting the war lies at the doorstep of both the political and the military echelons.

18. The overall image of the war was a result of a mixture of flawed conduct of the political and the military echelons and the interface between them, of flawed performance by the IDF, and especially the ground forces, and of deficient Israeli preparedness. Israel did not use its military force well and effectively, despite the fact that it was a limited war initiated by Israel itself. At the end of the day, Israel did not gain a political achievement because of military successes; rather, it relied on a political agreement, which included positive elements for Israel, which permitted it to stop a war which it had failed to win.

19. This outcome was primarily caused by the fact that, from the very beginning, the war has not been conducted on the basis of deep understanding of the theatre of operations, of the IDF's readiness and preparedness, and of basic principles of using military power to achieve a political and diplomatic goal.

20. All in all, the IDF failed, especially because of the conduct of the high command and the ground forces, to provide an effective military response to the challenge posed to it by the war in Lebanon, and thus failed to provide the political echelon with a military achievement that could have served as the basis for political and diplomatic action. Responsibility for this outcome lies mainly with the IDF, but the misfit between the mode of action and the goals determined by the political echelon share responsibility.

21. We should note that, alongside the failures in the IDF performance, there were also important military achievements. Special mention should go to the great willingness of the soldiers, especially reserve soldiers, to serve and fight in the war, as well as the many instances of heroism, courage, self-sacrifice and devotion of many commanders and soldiers.

22. The air force should be congratulated on very impressive achievements in this war. However, there were those in the IDF high command, joined by some in the political echelon, who entertained a baseless hope that the capabilities of the air force could prove

decisive in the war. In fact, the impressive achievements of the air force were necessarily limited, and were eroded by the weaknesses in the overall performance of the IDF.

23. The "Hannit" episode coloured to a large extent the whole performance of the Navy, despite the fact that it made a critical contribution to the naval blockade, and provided the Northern Command with varied effective support of its fighting.

24. We should also note that the war had significant diplomatic achievements. SC resolution 1701, and the fact it was adopted unanimously, were an achievement for Israel. This conclusion stands even if it turns out that only a part of the stipulations of the resolution were implemented or will be implemented, and even if it could have been foreseen that some of them would not be implemented. This conclusion also does not depend on the intentions or goals of the powers that supported the resolution.

25. We note, however, that we have seen no serious staff work on Israeli positions in the negotiations. This situation improved in part when the team headed by the prime minister's head of staff was established. The team worked efficiently and with dedication, professionalism and coordination. This could not compensate, however, for the absence of preparatory staff work and discussions in the senior political echelon.

26. This fact may have much significance to the way Israel conducts negotiations, and to the actual content of the arrangements reached. In such negotiations, decisions are often made that may have far-reaching implications on Israel's interests, including the setting of precedents.

27. The staff work done in the Ministry of Foreign Affairs concerning the adoption of a favourable resolution in the Security Council was, in the main, quick, systematic and efficient. At the same time, for a variety of reasons, it did not reflect clear awareness of the essential need to maintain an effective relationship between military achievements and diplomatic activities.

28. We now turn to the political and military activity concerning the ground operation at the end of the war. This is one of the central foci of public debate.

29. True, in hindsight, the large ground operation did not achieve its goals of limiting the rocket fire and changing the picture of the war. It is not clear what the ground operation contributed to speeding up the diplomatic achievement or improving it. It is also unclear to what extent starting the ground offensive affected the reactions of the government of Lebanon and Hezbollah to the ceasefire.

30. Nonetheless, it is important to stress that the evaluation of these decisions should not be made with hindsight. It cannot depend on the achievements or the costs these decisions in fact had. The evaluation must be based only on the reasons for the operation, and its risks and prospects as they were known—or as they should have been known—when it was decided upon. Moreover, it is impossible to evaluate the ground operation at the end of the war without recalling the developments that preceded it and the repeated delays in the adoption of the Security Council resolution; and as a part of the overall conduct of the war.

31. Against this background, we make the following findings on the main decisions:

- The cabinet decision of August 9th—to approve in principle the IDF plan, but to authorise the PM and the MOD to decide if and when it should be activated, according to the diplomatic timetable—was almost inevitable, giving the Israeli government necessary military and political flexibility.
- The decision to start in fact the ground operation was within the political and professional discretion of its makers, on the basis of the facts before them. The goals of the ground operation were legitimate, and were not exhausted by the wish to hasten or improve the diplomatic achievement. There was no failure in that decision in itself, despite its limited achievements and its painful costs.
- Both the position of the Prime minister—who had preferred to avoid the ground operation—and the position of the Minister of Defence—who had thought it would have served Israel's interest to go for it—had been taken on the merits and on the basis of evidence. Both enjoyed serious support among the members of the general staff of the IDF and others. Even if both statesmen took into account political and public concerns—a fact we cannot ascertain—we believe that they both acted out of a strong and

sincere perception of what they thought at the time was Israel's interest.

32. We want to stress: The duty to make these difficult decisions was the political leaders'. The sole test of these decisions is public and political.

33. At the same time, we also note that:

- We have not found within either the political or the military echelons a serious consideration of the question whether it was reasonable to expect military achievements in 60 hours that could have contributed meaningfully to any of the goals of the operation;
- We have not found that the political echelon was aware of the details of the fighting in real time, and we have not seen a discussion, in either the political or the military echelons, of the issue of stopping the military operation after the Security Council resolution was adopted;
- We have not seen an explanation of the tension between the great effort to get additional time to conclude the first stage of the planned ground operation and the decisions not to go on fighting until the ceasefire itself.

34. A description of failures in the conduct of war may be regarded as harming Israel. There will be those who may use our findings to hurt Israel and its army. We nonetheless point out these failures and shortcomings because we are certain that only in this way Israel may come out of this ordeal strengthened. We are pleased that processes of repair have already started. We recommend a deep and systematic continuation of such processes. It is exclusively in the hands of Israeli leaders and public to determine whether, when facing challenges in the future, we will come to them more prepared and ready, and whether we shall cope with them in a more serious and responsible way than the way the decision-makers had acted—in the political and the military echelons — in the 2nd Lebanon war.

35. Our recommendations contain suggestions for systemic and deep changes in the modalities of thinking and acting of the political and military echelons and their interface, in both routine and emergency, including war. These are deep and critical processes. Their significance should not be obscured by current affairs, local successes

or initial repairs. A persistent and prolonged effort, on many levels, will be needed in order to bring about the essential improvements in the ways of thinking and acting of the political-military systems.

36. For these reasons we would like to caution against dangers which might upset plans and delay required change processes, and thus produce dangerous results:

- Fear of criticism in case of failure may lead to defensive reactions, working by the book, and abstention from making resolute decisions and preferring non-action. Such behaviour is undesirable and also dangerous.
- In a dynamic complex reality, one should not prepare better for the last war. It is also essential not to limit oneself to superficial action, designed to create an appearance that flaws had been corrected.
- It is also essential not to focus exclusively on coping with dangers, but to combine readiness for threat scenarios with an active seeking of opportunities.
- When speaking on learning, one should take into account that enemies, too, are learning their lessons.

37. The 2nd Lebanon War has brought again to the foreground for thought and discussion issues that some parts of Israeli society had preferred to suppress: Israel cannot survive in this region, and cannot live in it in peace or at least non-war, unless people in Israel itself and in its surroundings believe that Israel has the political and military leadership, military capabilities, and social robustness that will allow her to deter those of its neighbours who wish to harm her, and to prevent them—if necessary through the use of military force—from achieving their goal.

38. These truths do not depend on one's partisan or political views. Israel must—politically and morally—seek peace with its neighbours and make necessary compromises. At the same time, seeking peace or managing the conflict must come from a position of social, political and military strength, and through the ability and willingness to fight for the state, its values and the security of its population even in the absence of peace.

39. These truths have profound and far-reaching implications for many

dimensions of life in Israel and the ways its challenges are managed. Beyond examining the way the Lebanon War was planned and conducted; beyond the examination of flaws in decision-making and performance that had been revealed in it—important as they may be; these are the central questions that the Lebanon war has raised. These are issues that lie at the very essence of our existence here as a Jewish and democratic state. These are the questions we need to concentrate on.

40. We hope that our findings and conclusions in the Interim and the Final Reports will bring about not only a redress of failings and flaws, but help Israeli society, its leaders and thinkers, to advance the long-term goals of Israel, and develop the appropriate ways to address the challenges and respond to them.

41. We are grateful for the trust put in us when this difficult task was given to us. If we succeed in facilitating rectification of the failings we have identified—this will be our best reward.

Appendix C

UN SECURITY COUNCIL RESOLUTION 1701

11 August 2006

The Security Council,

Recalling all its previous resolutions on Lebanon, in particular resolutions 425 (1978), 426 (1978), 520 (1982), 1559 (2004), 1655 (2006) 1680 (2006) and 1697 (2006), as well as the statements of its President on the situation in Lebanon, in particular the statements of 18 June 2000 (S/PRST/2000/21), of 19 October 2004 (S/PRST/2004/36), of 4 May 2005 (S/PRST/2005/17), of 23 January 2006 (S/PRST/2006/3) and of 30 July 2006 (S/PRST/2006/35),

Expressing its utmost concern at the continuing escalation of hostilities in Lebanon and in Israel since Hezbollah's attack on Israel on 12 July 2006, which has already caused hundreds of deaths and injuries on both sides, extensive damage to civilian infrastructure and hundreds of thousands of internally displaced persons,

Emphasising the need for an end of violence, but at the same time *emphasising* the need to address urgently the causes that have given rise to the current crisis, including by the unconditional release of the abducted Israeli soldiers,

Mindful of the sensitivity of the issue of prisoners and *encouraging* the efforts aimed at urgently settling the issue of the Lebanese prisoners detained in Israel,

Welcoming the efforts of the Lebanese Prime Minister and the commitment of the Government of Lebanon, in its seven-point plan, to extend its authority over its territory, through its own legitimate armed forces, such that there will be no weapons without the consent of the Government of Lebanon and no authority other than that of the Government of Lebanon, *welcoming also* its commitment to a United Nations force that is supplemented and enhanced in numbers, equipment, mandate and scope of operation, and *bearing in mind* its request in this plan for an immediate withdrawal of the Israeli forces from southern Lebanon,

Determined to act for this withdrawal to happen at the earliest,

Taking due note of the proposals made in the seven-point plan regarding the Shebaa farms area,

Welcoming the unanimous decision by the Government of Lebanon on 7 August 2006 to deploy a Lebanese armed force of 15,000 troops in South Lebanon as the Israeli army withdraws behind the Blue Line and to request the assistance of additional forces from UNIFIL as needed, to facilitate the entry of the Lebanese armed forces into the region and to restate its intention to strengthen the Lebanese armed forces with material as needed to enable it to perform its duties,

Aware of its responsibilities to help secure a permanent ceasefire and a long-term solution to the conflict,

Determining that the situation in Lebanon constitutes a threat to international peace and security,

1. *Calls for* a full cessation of hostilities based upon, in particular, the immediate cessation by Hezbollah of all attacks and the immediate cessation by Israel of all offensive military operations;
2. Upon full cessation of hostilities, *calls upon* the Government of Lebanon and UNIFIL as authorised by paragraph 11 to deploy their forces together throughout the South and *calls upon* the Government of Israel, as that deployment begins, to withdraw all of its forces from southern Lebanon in parallel;
3. *Emphasises* the importance of the extension of the control of the Government of Lebanon over all Lebanese territory in accordance with the provisions of resolution 1559 (2004) and resolution 1680 (2006), and of the relevant provisions of the Ta'if Accords, for it to exercise its full sovereignty, so that there will be no weapons without the consent of the Government of Lebanon and no authority other than that of the Government of Lebanon;
4. *Reiterates* its strong support for full respect for the Blue Line;
5. *Also reiterates* its strong support, as recalled in all its previous relevant resolutions, for the territorial integrity, sovereignty and political

independence of Lebanon within its internationally recognised borders, as contemplated by the Israeli-Lebanese General Armistice Agreement of 23 March 1949;

6. *Calls on* the international community to take immediate steps to extend its financial and humanitarian assistance to the Lebanese people, including through facilitating the safe return of displaced persons and, under the authority of the Government of Lebanon, reopening airports and harbours, consistent with paragraphs 14 and 15, and *calls on* it also to consider further assistance in the future to contribute to the reconstruction and development of Lebanon;

7. *Affirms* that all parties are responsible for ensuring that no action is taken contrary to paragraph 1 that might adversely affect the search for a long-term solution, humanitarian access to civilian populations, including safe passage for humanitarian convoys, or the voluntary and safe return of displaced persons, and *calls on* all parties to comply with this responsibility and to cooperate with the Security Council;

8. *Calls for* Israel and Lebanon to support a permanent ceasefire and a long-term solution based on the following principles and elements:

   - full respect for the Blue Line by both parties;—security arrangements to prevent the resumption of hostilities, including the establishment between the Blue Line and the Litani river of an area free of any armed personnel, assets and weapons other than those of the Government of Lebanon and of UNIFIL as authorised in paragraph 11, deployed in this area;
   - full implementation of the relevant provisions of the Taif Accords, and of resolutions 1559 (2004) and 1680 (2006), that require the disarmament of all armed groups in Lebanon, so that, pursuant to the Lebanese cabinet decision of 27 July 2006, there will be no weapons or authority in Lebanon other than that of the Lebanese State;
   - no foreign forces in Lebanon without the consent of its Government;
   - no sales or supply of arms and related materiel to Lebanon except as authorised by its Government;
   - provision to the United Nations of all remaining maps of land mines in Lebanon in Israel's possession;

9. *Invites* the Secretary-General to support efforts to secure as soon as possible agreements in principle from the Government of Lebanon and the Government of Israel to the principles and elements for a long-term solution as set forth in paragraph 8, and *expresses* its intention to be actively involved;

10. *Requests* the Secretary-General to develop, in liaison with relevant international actors and the concerned parties, proposals to implement the relevant provisions of the Taif Accords, and resolutions 1559 (2004) and 1680 (2006), including disarmament, and for delineation of the international borders of Lebanon, especially in those areas where the border is disputed or uncertain, including by dealing with the Shebaa farms area, and to present to the Security Council those proposals within thirty days;

11. *Decides*, in order to supplement and enhance the force in numbers, equipment, mandate and scope of operations, to authorise an increase in the force strength of UNIFIL to a maximum of 15,000 troops, and that the force shall, in addition to carrying out its mandate under resolutions 425 and 426 (1978):

    (a) Monitor the cessation of hostilities;

    (b) Accompany and support the Lebanese armed forces as they deploy throughout the South, including along the Blue Line, as Israel withdraws its armed forces from Lebanon as provided in paragraph 2;

    (c) Coordinate its activities related to paragraph 11(b) with the Government of Lebanon and the Government of Israel;

    (d) Extend its assistance to help ensure humanitarian access to civilian populations and the voluntary and safe return of displaced persons;

    (e) Assist the Lebanese armed forces in taking steps towards the establishment of the area as referred to in paragraph 8;

    (f) Assist the Government of Lebanon, at its request, to implement paragraph 14;

12. Acting in support of a request from the Government of Lebanon to deploy an international force to assist it to exercise its authority throughout the territory, *authorises* UNIFIL to take all necessary action in areas of deployment of its forces and as it deems within its capabilities, to ensure that its area of operations is not utilised for

hostile activities of any kind, to resist attempts by forceful means to prevent it from discharging its duties under the mandate of the Security Council, and to protect United Nations personnel, facilities, installations and equipment, ensure the security and freedom of movement of United Nations personnel, humanitarian workers and, without prejudice to the responsibility of the Government of Lebanon, to protect civilians under imminent threat of physical violence;

13. *Requests* the Secretary-General urgently to put in place measures to ensure UNIFIL is able to carry out the functions envisaged in this resolution, *urges* Member States to consider making appropriate contributions to UNIFIL and to respond positively to requests for assistance from the Force, and *expresses* its strong appreciation to those who have contributed to UNIFIL in the past;

14. *Calls upon* the Government of Lebanon to secure its borders and other entry points to prevent the entry in Lebanon without its consent of arms or related materiel and *requests* UNIFIL as authorised in paragraph 11 to assist the Government of Lebanon at its request;

15. *Decides* further that all States shall take the necessary measures to prevent, by their nationals or from their territories or using their flag vessels or aircraft:

    (a) The sale or supply to any entity or individual in Lebanon of arms and related materiel of all types, including weapons and ammunition, military vehicles and equipment, paramilitary equipment, and spare parts for the aforementioned, whether or not originating in their territories; and

    (b) The provision to any entity or individual in Lebanon of any technical training or assistance related to the provision, manufacture, maintenance or use of the items listed in subparagraph (a) above; except that these prohibitions shall not apply to arms, related material, training or assistance authorised by the Government of Lebanon or by UNIFIL as authorised in paragraph 11;

16. *Decides* to extend the mandate of UNIFIL until 31 August 2007, and *expresses its intention* to consider, in a later resolution, further enhancements to the mandate and other steps to contribute to the implementation of a permanent ceasefire and a long-term solution;

17. *Requests* the Secretary-General to report to the Council within one week on the implementation of this resolution and subsequently on a regular basis;
18. *Stresses* the importance of, and the need to achieve, a comprehensive, just and lasting peace in the Middle East, based on all its relevant resolutions including its resolutions 242 (1967) of 22 November 1967, 338 (1973) of 22 October 1973 and 1515 (2003) of 18 November 2003;
19. *Decides* to remain actively seized of the matter.

BIBLIOGRAPHY

Books

Adam Harmon, *Lonely Soldier: The Memoir of an American Soldier in the Israeli Army* (New York: Ballantine Books, 2006)

Amos Harel and Avi Issacharoff, *34 Days: Israel, Hizbullah, and the War in Lebanon* (New York: Palgrave MacMillan, 2006)

Andrew Exum, *Hizballah at War: A Military Assessment* (Washington, DC: Washington Institute for Near East Policy, 2006)

Augustus Richard Norton, *Hezbollah: A Short History* (Princeton: Princeton University Press, 2007)

Beate Hamizrachi, *The Emergence of the South Lebanon Security Belt: Major Saad Haddad and the Ties with Israel, 1975–1978* (New York: Praeger, 1988)

Benjamin S. Lambeth, *Air Operations in Israel's War against Hezbollah: Learning from Lebanon and Getting It Right in Gaza* (Santa Monica, CA: RAND Corporation, 2011)

B. H. Liddell Hart, *Strategy,* 2nd revised edn. (New York: Meridian, 1991)

Carl von Clausewitz, *On War*. Edited by Michael Howard and Peter Paret (Princeton, NJ: Princeton University Press, 1976)

Christopher Bellamy, *The Evolution of Modern Land Warfare: Theory and Practice*(London: Routledge, 1990)

David Makovsky and Jeffrey White, *Lessons and Implications of the Israel-Hezbollah War: A Preliminary Assessment* (Washington, DC: Washington Institute for Near East Policy, 2006)

Daniel Byman, *A High Price: The Triumphs and Failures of Israeli Counterterrorism* (New York: Oxford University Press, 2011)

Daniel Isaac Helmer, *Flipside of the COIN: Israel's Lebanese Incursion Between 1982–2000. The Long War Series Occasional Paper 21* (Fort Leavenworth, KS: Combat Studies Institute Press, 2006)

David Lesch, *The Arab-Israeli Conflict: A History* (New York: Oxford University Press, 2008)

Edward A. Smith, *Effects Based Operations: Applying Network Centric Warfare in Peace, Crisis, and War* (Washington DC: The Command and Control Research Program, 2002)

Eliyahu Winograd *et al.*, *Final Report*, Tel Aviv: The Inquiry Commission to Examine the Events of the Military Campaign in Lebanon 2006, 2008 [in Hebrew]

Frank G. Hoffman, *Conflict in the 21st Century: The Rise of Hybrid Wars* (Arlington, VA: Potomac Institute for Policy Studies, 2007)

Frederic C. Hof, *Galilee Divided: The Israel-Lebanon Frontier, 1916-1984* (Colorado: Westview Press, 1985)

Gilbert Achcar with Michel Warschawski, *The 33-Day War: Israel's War on Hezbollah in Lebanon and It's Consequences* (Boulder and London: Paradigm Publishers, 2007)

Giulio Douhet, *Command of the Air* (New York, Coward-McCann, 1942)

Hany T. Nakhleh, *The 2006 Israeli War on Lebanon: Analysis and Strategic Implications.* (Carlisle Barracks, PA: Army War College, 2007)

H.E. Chehabi, *Distant Relations: Iran and Lebanon in the last 500 years* (London: I.B. Tauris, 2006)

James J. F. Forest, ed., *Influence Warfare: How Terrorists and Governments Fight to Shape Perceptions in a War of Ideas* (Westport, Conn.: Praeger Security International, 2009)

John A. Lynn, *Battle: A History of Combat and Culture* (Boulder, CO: Westview Press, 2003)

John Laffin, *The War of Desperation: Lebanon 1982–85* (London: Osprey, 1985)

Judith Palmer Harik, *Hezbollah: The Changing Face of Terrorism* (London and New York, I.B.Tauris, 2005)

Kenneth J. Campbell, *A Tale of Two Quagmires: Iraq, Vietnam, and the Hard Lessons of War* (Boulder and London: Paradigm Publishers, 2007)

Martin van Creveld, *The Sword and the Olive: A Critical History of the Israeli Defence Force* (New York: Public Affairs, 1998)

Naim Qassem, *Hizbullah: The Story from Within*. Translated by Dalia Khalil (London: SAQI, 2005)

Nicholas Blanford, *Warriors of God: Inside Hezbollah's Thirty-Year Struggle with Israel* (New York: Random House, 2011)

Nicholas Noe, ed., *Voice of Hezbollah: The Statements of Sayyed Hassan Nasrallah* (London: Verso, 2007)

Richard A. Gabriel, *Operation Peace for Galilee: The Israeli-PLO War in Lebanon* (New York: Hill and Wang, 1985)

Robert Baer, *The Devil We Know* (New York: Random House, 2008)

Robert Fisk, *Pity the Nation—Lebanon at War*, 3rd edn., (Oxford, Oxford University Press, 2001)

Robert Pape, *Bombing to Win: Air Power and Coercion in War* (Ithaca, N.Y.: Cornell Univ. Press, 1996)

Rupert Smith, *The Utility of Force: The Art of War in the Modern World* (New York: Vintage Books, 2005)

Shlomo Brom and Meir Elan, eds., *The Second Lebanon War: Strategic Perspectives* (Tel Aviv: Institute for National Security Studies, 2007)

Shmuel Gordon, *The Vulture and the Snake: Counter-Guerrilla Air Warfare: The War in Southern Lebanon*(Ramat Gan: Begin-Sadat Center for Strategic Studies, Bar-Ilan University, 1998)

Stephen Biddle, *Military Power: Explaining Victory and Defeat in Modern Battle* (Princeton: Princeton University Press, 2004)

Thanassis Cambanis, *A Privilege to Die: Inside Hezbollah's Legions and Their Endless War with Israel* (New York: Free Press, 2010)

The Commission for the Examination of the Events of the 2006 Campaign in Lebanon, *The Second Lebanon War: Final Report*, Vol. I, January 2008

Thomas Collelo, *Lebanon: A Country Study* (Washington DC: Federal Research Division, Library of Congress, 1987)

Thomas X. Hammes, *The Sling and the Stone: On War in the 21st Century*, St. Paul, MN: Zenith Press, 2004.

William M. Arkin, *Divining Victory: Airpower in the 2006 Israel-Hezbollah War* (Maxwell Air Force Base, AL: Air University Press, 2007)

William L. Cleveland, *The History of Modern Middle East* (Boulder, Westview Press, 1994)

William W. Harris, *Faces of Lebanon: Sects, Wars, and Global Extensions* (Princeton, NJ: Markus Wiener Publishers, 1997)

Zeev Schiff, *A History of the Israeli Army 1874 To The Present* (New York: Macmillan Publishing Company, 1985)

Published Articles/Monographs

Anthony H. Cordesman, George Sullivan, and William D. Sullivan, "Lessons of the 2006 Israeli-Hezbollah War," *Significant Issues Series* 29, no. 4 (Washington, D.C.: CSIS Press, 2007)

Alon Ben-David, "Lebanon War Report Reproaches Israeli Leaders." *Jane's Defence Weekly*, Vol. 44, No. 19, May 2007.

Augustus Richard Norton, "Hizballah and the Israeli Withdrawal from Southern Lebanon." *Journal of Palestine Studies*, Vol. 30, No. 1, Autumn 2000.

Augustus Richard Norton and Jillian Schwedler. "(In)Security Zones in South Lebanon." *Journal of Palestine Studies*, Vol. 23, No. 1, Autumn 1993.

Benjamin S. Lambeth, *Air Operations in Israel's War against Hezbollah: Learning from Lebanon and Getting it Right in Gaza* (Santa Monica, CA: RAND Corporation, 2011), p. 113, http://www.rand.org/pubs/monographs/MG835.html.

Captain Daniel Helmer, "Not Quite Counterinsurgency: A Cautionary Tale for US Forces Based on Israel's Operation Change of Direction." *Armour,* January–February 2007.

Efraim Inbar, "How Israel Bungled the Second Lebanon War." *Middle East Quarterly*, Summer 2007.

Matt M. Mathews, "We Were Caught Unprepared: The 2006 Hezbollah-Israeli War", U.S. Army Combined Arms Center, *Long War Series Occasional Paper 26*; OP 26; usacac.army.mil/cac2/cgsc/carl/download/csipubs/matthewsOP26.pdf

Max Boot, "The Second Lebanon War." *Weekly Standard,* September 2006.

Milan N. Vego, "Effects-Based Operations: A Critique." *JFQ*, No. 41, 2nd Quarter, 2006.

Nahum Barnea, "Israel vs. Hezbollah." *Foreign Policy,* November–December 2006.

Mordechai Nisan, "Did Israel Betray Its Lebanese Allies?" *Middle East Quarterly*, December, 2000.

Martha Wenger and Julie Denney. "Lebanon's Fifteen-Year War 1975–1990." *Middle East Report*, No. 162, January–February 1990.

Sarah E. Kreps, "The 2006 Lebanon War: Lessons Learned." *Parameters,* Vol. XXXVII, No. 1, Spring 2007.

Shmuel L. Gordon, "The Vulture and the Snake: Counter-Guerrilla Air Warfare: The War in Southern Lebanon." *Mideast Security and Policy Studies*, No. 39, July 1998.

INDEX